MINDFULNESS
MEDITATIONS
for
ANXIETY

100 SIMPLE PRACTICES TO
FIND PEACE RIGHT NOW

Michael Smith, PhD

ALTHEA
PRESS

For general information on our other products and services or to obtain technical support, please contact our Customer Care Department within the U.S. at (866) 744-2665, or outside the U.S. at (510) 253-0500.

Althea Press publishes its books in a variety of electronic and print formats. Some content that appears in print may not be available in electronic books, and vice versa.

Interior and Cover Designer: Michael Patti
Art Producer: Sara Feinstein
Editor: Emily Angell
Production Editor: Andrew Yackira

All art used under license from Shutterstock.com and iStock.com

Author photo courtesy of © Chad Morgan Photography

ISBN: Print 978-1-64152-484-1 | eBook 978-1-64152-485-8

DEDICATED TO
my incredible wife,
Padma, to my Tibetan
Teacher, and to the
alleviation of people's
suffering

CONTENTS

"MEDITATE …
DO NOT DELAY,
LEST YOU LATER
REGRET IT."

—The Buddha

INTRODUCTION

WHEN I WAS YOUNG, I was smaller than most of the other boys and pretty skinny. My small size, combined with a significant stutter, led to frequent tormenting and bullying by other kids and resulted in considerable anxiety and avoidance on my part. This high anxiety followed me through high school and into college, although the anxiety I felt about the stutter persisted into my 50s.

Another source of significant anxiety in my life centers around some of the many sports that I have participated in, including many extreme sports. While I enjoy the challenge of these sports, including rock climbing, scuba diving, skydiving, white water running, mountain biking, solo backpacking, and martial arts, they all entail confronting and managing a significant amount of fear and anxiety.

A third source of anxiety, and perhaps the most debilitating, was when I had a serious illness 6 or 7 years ago, resulting in fairly urgent open abdominal surgery. I was quite ill; it happened quickly and unexpectedly, and my support resources were very limited. I was extremely weak afterwards, and it took a long time to really recover, though I still needed to return to work and perform at a high level. This experience completely changed my lifestyle, rattled my confidence, brought up an enormous amount of fear and futility, and resulted in an extended period of severe anxiety, including anxiety attacks.

Slowly, I was able to work through all of this, using most of the same techniques that I will be teaching you. In short, I have faced and dealt with an enormous amount of fear and anxiety for much of my life. The need to understand and heal myself of this omnipresent anxiety was undoubtedly a main reason that I went into psychology, though not the only one.

Pretty early on I knew that I wanted to be a psychologist, and I completed multiple graduate degrees and numerous certifications, all in various areas of psychology. I have worked for over 40 years as a psychotherapist and clinical and transpersonal psychologist. My intention in working with my clients is to help them get what they most need and want in life, which is usually to be genuinely happy, enjoy loving relationships, be successful in work and life, and minimize their suffering. I really love what I do.

I received my first formal training in meditation in 1969 when Transcendental Meditation was in vogue. I took the basic course and had some success with it, and this motivated me to go on to study most of the various types of meditation that are found in the great religions. These include Hindu absorption states and yoga asanas, Shamanistic ritual and nature meditation, Islamic and Sufi Zikr and dancing, Christian contemplation and prayer, Taoist nature and internal meditation, Judaic rituals and singing, and all forms of Buddhist meditation. In 1978, I went to my first mindfulness meditation retreat, and I have attended numerous mindfulness meditation retreats ever since. In September 1983, I met my first Tibetan Rinpoche and began studying Tibetan Buddhism. I have completed dozens of Tibetan Buddhist meditation retreats since then, and I still go on at least one retreat a year.

Of all the various things that I have done to better myself, heal, and grow, I consider meditation to be the single most important and valuable. Meditation has helped me calm my mind, emotions, and body. It has enabled me to work through an enormous amount of fear and bad memories and given me the ability to do "psychotherapy" on myself as problems arise.

A particular form of meditation that I will be sharing with you—I call it "Feel your body and breathe" (page 210)—actually saved my life when a friend of mine and I were scuba diving in a large lake with near-zero visibility and became lost under a sunken overpass. We could see only two inches in front of our faces and had limited air. The only way to survive was to stay calm, not panic, control our air use, and hopefully find our way out of there. I have never been so happy to break the surface of the water in my life!

Finally, and perhaps most important, meditation has given me a clear insight into and direct experience of my true nature. All of these benefits are available to you, too, if you begin to study and earnestly practice meditation.

This book is about teaching you meditation; mindfulness-based meditation in particular, including the various steps, stages, and applications, and how to use meditation to combat anxiety. Meditation is relatively simple, very inexpensive, does not take any special equipment, and can be done anywhere and anytime.

There is one caveat: To learn and become proficient at meditation, you must commit to studying and practicing it. Studying meditation includes going over the exercises and learning the basic steps, so you can eventually do basic meditation and apply it without any prompts. Practicing meditation is the actual application of the instructions regularly and over time. I'll be helping you with that, and you'll learn all the tools you need to get started, make progress, apply mindfulness meditation to your everyday life and anxieties, and hopefully welcome increased calm and clarity into your life. I have included 100 meditations in this book to provide many options for you to use meditation in your daily life, regardless of the amount of time you have and whether you generally feel calm or really anxious.

The primary goal of this book is to teach you mindfulness meditation, to provide you with proven and reliable resources you can refer to and use anytime and anyplace, and to help you calm your mind, emotions, and body, thus greatly reducing your anxiety, discomfort, and suffering, and enabling you to live life more fully and with greater happiness.

UNDERSTANDING MINDFULNESS, MEDITATION, *and* ANXIETY

I'll begin with an introduction to mindfulness and meditation in general. You'll learn where mindfulness comes from, common questions and answers about meditation, how to use it in conjunction with proven approaches in psychology, and what types of results you can expect. We will also go over some of the best practices in learning and applying mindfulness and psychology to overcome anxiety.

What Is Mindfulness?

First, a bit of history. Mindfulness is a form of meditation that primarily comes out of the Buddhist Theravada tradition, though elements of it are also found in Zen Buddhism and some in Tibetan Buddhism. Western Buddhist Vipassana meditation evolved from the Buddhist Theravada tradition, and the mindfulness movement comes from that.

In Buddhist meditation, there are three yanas, or vehicles. This refers to modes of spiritual practice and schools of Buddhism. These include Hinayana, the basic or foundational vehicle; Mahayana, the second or great vehicle; and Vajrayana, the third, also known as the diamond or tantric vehicle. As one goes through the vehicles, the later ones build on and incorporate the elements of each other. The stages of spiritual development in the Hinayana are calm abiding, or Shamatha, and clear seeing, or Vipashyana, which includes non-self. In the Mahayana vehicle, one adds bodhicitta, and emptiness of things, or Shunyata. In Vajrayana, one desires to train this mind of ours and develop pure perception, to experience the true nature of mind and clear light.

Mindfulness meditation is associated with the first yana, or vehicle, and mindfulness is unique in that it takes and incorporates the techniques of Buddhist attention and mind training but strips away the religious trappings, beliefs, ceremony, and vows. It is not affiliated with any religion. By studying mindfulness meditation, you gain the tools, skills, and benefits of mind training without any of the religious obligations.

Admittedly, some of this may sound quite foreign and abstract, but the actual process of mindfulness is usually very simple. Mindfulness is simply paying attention, noticing without judgment, and being present in whatever you're doing. As most people go about their daily lives, their minds wander to other thoughts or sensations, instead of being present with the actual activities they are participating in. Through mindfulness practice, we learn to be actively and more fully involved in these activities instead of allowing our minds to wander.

WHY MINDFULNESS WORKS

Mindfulness meditation provides you with the ability to train your mind to focus and maintain your attention, to remain in the present moment or nowness, and to approach life events and whatever arises in your mind or in the world with an open, non-judgmental, and caring attitude. The more we are aware of the present moment, firmly grounded in it, and acting from it, the better life is in all regards. Whatever we are doing, we become better at it.

What Is Meditation?

There are a number of possible definitions of meditation, and we will look at several of them. Meditation is an activity, usually connected with spirituality and found in all of the great religions, designed to transform the mind and heart and sometimes the body, and the goal is to move towards and through the stages of self-realization or enlightenment. There are many different forms of meditation, including concentration, openness, analysis, insight, awareness, clarity, calmness, self-love, compassion, visualization, chanting, and movement.

Meditation is a process through which we get to know how our mind works and train our attention to remain where we place it. My teacher used to say that his mind and attention were as "steady and stable as a cup sitting on a table!" By practicing meditation, we can get used to remaining present, undisturbed by whatever thoughts, emotions, or sensations arise. Our mind remains focused and steady. In its most simple form, meditation is just focusing our attention on something, in the here and now, and maintaining our attention, largely undistracted.

Meditation is about learning to simply be present with whatever arises in our mind and awareness. As things arise, we find ourselves able to remain more neutral and not identify with or grasp onto them. This is especially helpful in the arising of troubling thoughts, upsetting emotions, and unsettling sensations.

In meditation, there are things to gain and things to eliminate, and these usually happen simultaneously. For example, we need to develop our focus and concentration and eliminate our distractions and discursive thinking. As some develop, others naturally fall away. We need to gain compassion, love, and acceptance (for ourselves and others) and to let go of loathing, judgment, criticism, anger, and hate (for ourselves and others).

In meditation, we have the opportunity to examine our thoughts and emotions, our motivations, our actions and reactions, and the way in which we see the world. We actually get to discover who we really are.

WHY MEDITATION WORKS

All great religions, and most likely all cultures, have their own forms of meditation, and different types of meditation have been in existence for literally thousands of years. Mindfulness meditation, derived from Buddhism, has been in existence for about 2,600 years. Hindu and Taoist meditations have some similarities and have been around for approximately 4,000 and 2,000 years, respectively. While Tibetan Buddhism has not been in existence for that long, it was so integrated into their entire culture and daily life that everything revolved around it, thus speeding its development. Also, the "best and brightest" in the Tibetan culture were selected to study and develop the areas of meditation and spirituality. Instead of their high achievers becoming doctors, lawyers, CEOs, or politicians, they became spiritual scholars and meditation masters, strongly elevating and developing the field of meditation. Mindfulness meditation is simple, straightforward, well researched, and imminently practical.

Mindfulness for Anxiety: A New Model for Treatment

Regularly engaging in mindfulness meditation has been shown to significantly reduce anxiety, as well as stress and other negative or difficult emotions. However, the combination of therapies and mindfulness meditation you will learn in this book is something entirely new—it has not been presented before. It comes out of the culmination of my four decades of education, training, experience, and the synthesis of numerous fields of study and methods of psychotherapy. I've used it myself and with hundreds of clients over many years and get frequent reports as to its effectiveness.

As I mentioned earlier, mindfulness and meditation can occur anytime we focus our attention, largely undistracted. For example, you can focus on your breath, emotion, sensation, movement, the sky, nature, a picture, a candle, and so on. What we're doing here is using various methods to work with anxiety.

Let's take a look at the theory first. In traditional psychotherapy, we often focus on the story of the circumstances, and the thoughts we are having about the circumstances. For example, perhaps someone is dealing with a divorce and the idea of how they will cope with the financial or emotional burden of living alone. Some therapies then add in awareness of the emotions and suggestions on how to manage them. This might include awareness of anxiety or stress and then therapy and meditation suggested as management tools. In the somatic, or body-based, approaches to psychology, one may encounter and focus on various physical experiences. The individual might explore why their hands shake or their heart pounds when they enter the courtroom or see their spouse. However, these physical experiences are often not well integrated with the other two approaches that focus on thoughts and emotions because we don't usually think of sensations as having much importance in psychotherapy and healing. This approach is still relatively new.

I suggest that we consider that psychological issues exist simultaneously on all three levels. The mind, located in the head, is the center of thoughts and cognition. The heart is the center of emotions and love and is located in the center of the chest, while the body is the center of energy and power and is primarily located in the lower abdomen (though it includes the entire body). The mind center corresponds to thinking and telling the story about things. The heart center corresponds to various troubling emotions as well as love and compassion. The body center corresponds to energy and power and also includes any physical experiences throughout the body.

The major problem is that we tend to live our life in our head, in our thoughts and stories, cut off from our actual experience. Just like when we go out to eat, the menu is not the food, and when we're out and about, the map is not the actual territory, the thoughts about our experience is not the experience itself. We get lost in our mental ruminations and incessant worrying, and we miss the actual *experience*. We must put aside the digressive thinking and be mindful and aware of our actual emotional and physical experiences as they occur. This shift is the basis for what comes next: how to directly work with these experiences and transform them.

What actually shifts, lessens, and dissolves troubling emotions and physical experiences is the mindful awareness of them in the moment. Please reread that statement and think about it, as this is so very important. This is the basis for how meditation works in many of the great religions of the world: just being aware of our thoughts, emotions, and physical experiences with a focused but spacious awareness allows them to transform. This may take the form of changing, dissolving, lessening, or gaining insight about them. I remember the moment that I discovered this, and it was a life-altering moment for me. This fundamental approach has been providing psychological help and relief for people for thousands of years.

There are some old adages that point to this such as: "Be with what is, moment by moment," and "What you can be with, will let you be, and what you can't be with, won't let you be." Let's explore what the term "be with" is referring to, as this is both the crux of the matter and the heart of mindfulness meditation. We get lost in our mind's ruminative thinking, going around and around and stirring our anxiety higher and higher. We only make things worse. We believe that if we can only understand the problem, then it will be solved. This is especially prevalent in our very mentalistic, cognitively oriented, and generally well-educated culture.

Unfortunately, it is just not true. The way out of this conundrum is to simply be aware, moment by moment, of our actual emotional and physical experiences, as well as aware of our thoughts. This awareness of the experiences combined with the act of staying with them allows troubling experiences and problems to shift and dissolve. It is both my belief and experience that this is exactly how it works.

I further suggest that we should use this fundamental approach in combination with some of the most effective practices of modern psychology.

COMBINING THERAPIES

In psychology, a few therapies are recognized to be particularly effective. These include such modalities as cognitive behavioral therapy (CBT), EMDR (eye movement desensitization reprocessing), and the use of mindfulness. In addition to these, I use somatic focusing, which is the noticing of physical locations and sensations, as well as directing the breath into, through, or around these areas and sensations. My specific approach to breathing is derived from decades of studying breathwork, a Westernized form of breathing, similar to Kundalini yoga, but non-religious and significantly modified to provide a gentle and very safe approach to working with issues. The combination of these modalities has proven to be very effective and teachable. I get regular reports from clients as to how they use this approach, the various issues and situations they utilize it with, and the consistent results they achieve.

One other important thing that I do is add spaciousness to the mindfulness meditation. Typically, a mindfulness meditation is more of a concentrative meditation, where we mostly emphasize the ability to focus the mind, and as such, it has more involvement with thoughts. The main type of meditation that I do, Buddhist Dzogchen meditation, emphasizes awareness, spaciousness, and resting in that. When this type of approach is used on anxiety, the effects are multiplied exponentially. Many clients are able to focus their minds on their experiences, gently breathe into and through the sensations, allow the emotions to simply be there, and rest in the open space with it. It's a very calming and peaceful practice as well as an incredibly effective one.

Finally, I include many other types of therapy in conjunction with the therapy I just described as the fundamental skill or approach. As things begin to change to a more open and relaxed feeling, I find it is a really good time to include CBT therapy. Otherwise, it is like trying to teach someone to swim when they are deathly afraid of the water. One must get rid of some of the excessive negative emotion for the cognitive piece to really be effective. Eventually, most clients gain some expertise in finding a more mentally and emotionally open place while being with their experiences, and then they can reason with themselves in healthy and appropriate ways.

HOW MINDFULNESS MEDITATIONS EASE ANXIETY

Research on meditation in general began in the late 1960s with the Transcendental Meditation movement and has steadily progressed from there. Today, a considerable amount of scientific research exists regarding why and how meditation works, much of which has come out over the last three decades and especially the last ten years.

When we look at neuroscience in particular, scientists have been studying the physical effects of meditation for about 20 years using MRIs and other techniques. Research on neuroplasticity indicates that the human brain does not go into decline after a few decades of life, as was originally thought, but can change and evolve throughout adulthood and even into old age. We can form new connections and neurons, while learning new skills and engaging in mental challenges, throughout our life span.

Interesting research results reveal what happens inside the brain and how the brain changes with meditation. Mindfulness meditation appears to activate and increase the density of certain areas, while decreasing the activity and size of others. Some of the main areas that are activated and increase in density include the following:

> **INSULA:** associated with compassion, self-awareness, and empathy

> **LEFT HIPPOCAMPUS:** essential for memory. Helps us learn by increasing cognitive ability and recall, as well as increasing self-awareness, empathy, and emotional regulation.

> **PUTAMEN:** involved in learning

> **INTERIOR CINGULATE CORTEX:** regulates heart rate, blood pressure, breathing, and other autonomic functions

> **POSTERIOR CINGULATE:** associated with discursive thoughts and self-relevance (the amount of subjectivity and self-referral when processing information). The larger and stronger the posterior cingulate is, the fewer wandering and discursive thoughts we will have and the more realistic our sense of self will be. This area increases our ability to stay aware of the present moment, without judgment, and to observe such things as sensations and emotions that rise in the moment without overly identifying with them.

> **PREFRONTAL CORTEX:** mediates more complex thinking skills such as planning, decision-making, and self-regulating our social behavior

> **PONS:** where many of the neurotransmitters are produced. Regulates essential functions including facial expressions, sleep, basic physical functioning, and processing sensory input.

> **TEMPOROPARIETAL JUNCTION (TPJ):** associated with empathy and compassion, being humane and just, as well as our sense of perspective. This area becomes more active when we place ourselves in someone else's shoes, thus seeing and feeling things from their perspective.

I saved one of the most important areas for last: the amygdala. The previously mentioned brain areas all increase in activity, as well as size and gray matter density, but the amygdala is the one area of the brain that, when it changes through meditation, actually shrinks. This area of the brain produces feelings of anxiety, fear, reactivity, and general stress—and it is physically smaller in the brains of expert meditators.

Even just eight weeks of regular meditation can lead to a measurable decrease in the size of the amygdala. A smaller amygdala is associated with fewer strong emotional responses such as anxiety and "fight or flight." Changes in the brain caused by even a relatively small amount of meditation can leave us feeling significantly calmer and less anxious, with an increased sense of well-being.

On a whole-body level, some common effects of meditation include reduced pulse, lowered and more stable blood pressure, better sleep and reduced insomnia, increased cognition and recall, and reduced levels of cortisol, a hormone related to stress and adrenal fatigue. There are also numerous reports that show meditation reducing the amount of pain medication needed. One recent study showed that taking a break to practice mindfulness meditation was even better than a walk in nature for relaxing, refreshing, and revitalizing oneself.

Here is a final, short anecdotal story regarding my own experience with the effects of meditation. A couple of years ago, I was lying on a gurney in the procedure room awaiting a routine colonoscopy. I was connected to vitals monitoring and was being quizzed by the anesthesiologist to determine the amount of sedative Propofol to give me. He suddenly asked me if I had taken any anti-anxiety or other mood-altering medications prior to my arrival. I told him that I had not, and I expected him to move on with the questioning. However, he persisted, assuring me that it was "really okay if I had, but I just need to know," so that he could factor that into the anesthesia dose. Again, I assured him that I had not, at which time he paused and explained that my blood pressure was only 103/62 and pulse was 61, and that in all of his years of medical practice he had never had somebody with such low vital stats when they were about to undergo such a procedure. With a puzzled look, he glanced down and queried, "Okay, so what's your secret?" I looked up at him, smiled gently, and replied, "I meditate." He looked back at me with a big grin, shook his head, and exclaimed, "Wow, nice!"

Practicing (What Does It Mean to Practice Meditation?)

Practicing meditation describes engaging in and studying meditation regularly. It connotes something that is ongoing, a regular part of one's life, and a process, rather than a final destination. Meditation has no end-point. In light of this, it is useful to keep an idea of "process versus goal" in mind and focus on the journey, rather than being goal-oriented and striving for perfection, which can impede your meditation practice.

Ideally, meditation should be practiced daily. I recommend getting up in the morning and meditating immediately for at least a few minutes, with 15 to 30 minutes being ideal. It's so nice to begin the day with a calm, clear, and alert mind, and with attention focused but also spacious, like being out in nature. I also recommend taking short breaks from your day to meditate to come back to center and calm the mind and body. Night-time, especially right before bed, is another fine time to meditate. Every moment of meditation adds up.

AM I MEDITATING YET? (ANSWERS TO COMMON QUESTIONS)

Here are answers to some common questions about meditation.

WHEN WILL I START TO FEEL BETTER?

This question has a few answers. Generally, you will feel better almost immediately, and most new meditators notice at least some measure of increased relaxation, calmness, and sense of well-being after the first time they meditate. You may not feel a huge difference initially, but the effects are cumulative and clearly discernible over time.

A second answer is that "feeling better" comes and goes; some meditation sessions will seem successful while others can feel quite difficult and even like a waste of time. Long ago, my meditation teacher told me, "Don't worry about judging how you are doing and what is successful or not; just sit regularly, don't judge, and you will make steady progress."

The final answer is that there are stages to meditation, as well as levels of proficiency and attainment. The longer and more diligently we practice, the greater the amount of internal purification that occurs, the easier it is to settle our mind and drop our worrying thoughts, and the more open, profound, and far-reaching the results will be.

We can make progress as long as we continue meditating. His Holiness the Dalai Lama, though he is definitely enlightened and qualifies as a "living Buddha," spends the first four hours of every day, from 4 a.m. to 8 a.m., meditating, chanting, and studying. I find that very impressive, and learning this gave me an entirely new perspective on meditation practice.

HOW DO I KNOW IF I'M MEDITATING OR JUST SITTING THERE?

This is a good question, and at least initially it may be a bit difficult to discern this. There are a couple of things to look at: the first being your intention, which is to meditate, and the second being the activity that you are engaged in, that of sitting quietly for a certain amount of time as you watch your breath. As you progress, your depth of meditation increases, your alacrity in getting settled becomes easier and quicker, and it becomes clear that something really is happening. Try to just sit and meditate without judging or evaluating how well you think it's going.

AM I SUPPOSED TO THINK WHILE I'M MEDITATING?

It's very hard not to think, and if we try to forcefully control our mind and not think, it usually sets up a losing battle. Although in some of the more advanced stages of meditation one may have moments or even extended periods where they have no thoughts, this is definitely not our initial goal as beginners.

WHAT IF I KEEP FALLING ASLEEP?

When you find yourself frequently falling asleep while meditating, examine the following: You may be tired and not getting sufficient quality sleep at night. If this is the case, then you will naturally doze off when you quiet your mind and settle. When I was learning my first meditation style, Transcendental Meditation, I was having this issue. My teacher pointedly suggested, "Michael, you need to sleep at night, so you don't nap instead of meditating! And by the way, if you sit up straighter, breathe more deeply and strongly, and keep your eyes open, these will likely prevent this. Oh, and by the way, never, ever try to meditate while lying down with your eyes shut!" To this I would add, try meditating earlier in the day versus late at night. Finally, you may find yourself quite sleepy and have a hard time staying awake when you are beginning to enter very deep stages of meditation, where mind and body are becoming quite relaxed. During this stage, old fatigue may be clearing out, or you may simply become very mentally relaxed, and you struggle with staying awake. But dozing is not meditating, so keep in mind these suggestions.

WHAT IS THE BEST MEDITATION POSITION?

Sit comfortably, with your spine straight but relaxed, and breathe naturally. You don't have to sit on the floor; you may sit in a chair, and there are also meditations for standing and moving. Make sure you are comfortable when you sit and not in pain. We will cover this in more detail in the exercises section.

WHAT DO I DO IF MY MIND WANDERS?

Rest assured that your mind will wander. When it does, and you notice it, gently but firmly turn your attention back to your breath or whatever you are focusing on. One of the main reasons we do meditation, and particularly mindfulness meditation, is to train ourselves to be able to focus, especially on the breath, and to rid ourselves of a wandering mind.

WHEN IS THE BEST TIME TO MEDITATE? MORNING, EVENING, OR SOME OTHER TIME?

General consensus is that the best time to meditate is first thing in the morning, and especially the early morning, as there are fewer distractions when we are fresh. I think it's also good to meditate in the evening, especially before bed, to wind down, calm, and settle oneself. Another good time to meditate is whenever we are feeling stressed, worried, or agitated. It's surprising what even a few minutes of mindfulness meditation can do to calm and settle us. The final answer is that any time that you can get yourself to sit and meditate is a very good time to do so!

HOW LONG SHOULD ONE MEDITATE? HOW MUCH TIME IS NEEDED?

The answer really varies. When one is first beginning to meditate, even a few minutes can seem like a very long time. As you progress and get acquainted with the meditative state, you can sustain longer and longer periods of meditation without much discomfort. In the beginning, I think it's good to start with something simple like 3 to 5 minutes, take a break, and then return to the meditation. Often in meditation instruction, a teacher will suggest 20 to 30 minutes, although as my teacher has said, "There is nothing in the sutras and nothing magical about 20 to 30 minutes of meditation." He went on to say, "In the beginning, it will probably feel difficult, but if you persist, you may reach the stage where even many hours a day is not a burden. And, ultimately, you may find yourself in a perpetual state of meditation all day long." What he alluded to is that being in a mindful and meditative state all of the time is a real possibility and actually the goal, though it's usually unspoken. To achieve this state, you generally need to meditate regularly and build up to longer periods of time. My teacher recently suggested that all his students should meditate for an hour every day.

DO I NEED TO MEDITATE EVERY DAY?

Ideally, yes, it is best to get in the habit of meditating every day or even a few times a day every day. A daily practice will give you the best result, no matter which meditation you do.

CAN I MEDITATE WHILE WALKING AND RUNNING?

Yes! Applying ongoing mindfulness and awareness to any activity or object can be considered meditating, and this includes feeling our body and feet as we move through space and engage in activities. Consider how accomplished Michael Jordan was at participating in sports with mindfulness and awareness. Few people realize that he studied Zen Buddhist meditation with Phil Jackson, his coach, who was a proponent of Zen meditation, and Jordan was applying it to his basketball game. His proficiency in mindfulness meditation, paired with his strong presence, work ethic, skill level, and ability to be fully in the moment as he played the game at a high level, made him so incredibly good. Similarly, Tiger Woods, especially in his early days, was practicing Buddhist meditation that was taught to him by his uncle, a Buddhist monk, and this enabled him to excel far beyond others in the field.

Most people are not aware that martial arts, in addition to being tremendous exercise, excellent self-defense, and good for confidence, are actually meditative in nature and specifically designed to develop mindfulness, awareness, compassion, strength, and energy. These are some of reasons that I so loved doing martial arts and practiced it for many decades. Fairly early on, I discovered these hidden qualities and was able to begin to apply them in all situations; to this day, I still use mindfulness and body awareness practices that I discovered and developed during my years of formal martial arts practice. Currently I study and practice Tai chi and qigong and enjoy the fact that it is based on these same principles.

Many of the questions here will be addressed in the exercises section of the book, and you will have the opportunity to discover many of these things for yourself.

This book is designed to give you an excellent foundation in mindfulness meditation and show you how to apply it to various areas of your life. I suggest you begin with the most basic meditations and develop a solid familiarity with them. If you wish to progress a bit further with mindfulness meditation, there are several exercises that develop even stronger mindfulness. Use your skills to engage in any of the subsequent meditations.

I've included exercises for many areas of life and situations. Once you have the basic mindfulness meditation skill down, explore the book and sections as you need or have an interest. Find an exercise that interests you. Read though the introduction and the steps. Keep the book handy to refer to as you do the exercise, if needed. As you follow the steps, note your experience and results. All exercises are stand-alone, and some are also sequential in their development. Relax, try them out, and see what works for you and what brings you relief and ease. You may wish to make notes following the exercises. The more you use these exercises, the better and faster the results will be, so keep coming back often. I truly hope that you enjoy and benefit from the exercises and this book.

> "Life is a dance. Mindfulness is witnessing that dance."
> —Amit Ray

PART ONE

CALM *the* MIND

1

Basic mindfulness meditation

TIME: 15 MINUTES

Let's get right to it and give you the basics of mindfulness meditation; this exercise contains all of the fundamentals. You can come back to this exercise over and over as you continue to learn.

When learning mindfulness meditation, there are a few fundamental things you should pay particular attention to. The first is how you are sitting, which can be on the floor, on a cushion, or in a chair, and the spine should be straight but relaxed. The next thing you'll do is find your breath, wherever you are most aware of it, and simply observe it without trying to alter it. Finally, you'll move your attention to your breathing in the nose or the nostril area. Let's try it.

STEPS

1   Find a comfortable place to sit where you won't be disturbed and where you can focus on the exercise, ideally for the next 10 to 15 minutes.

2   Sit with your spine fairly straight but relaxed. You may sit with your eyes open or closed, whichever you prefer.

3   Breathe normally, noticing where you find the breath, and then bring your attention to your breath at the nostrils.

4   Be aware of your breath, and notice/follow it as you breathe in and out.

5   If or when your thoughts wander, just return your attention to your breath at the nostrils.

6   Continue to focus on your breath, perhaps sitting for 3 minutes the first time. Then, take a short break, and sit again for 5 minutes the second time. If you're feeling bold, take another very short break and then sit again for another 5 minutes.

7   Please congratulate yourself and go about your day. You may find it useful to keep notes as to when you meditated, for how long, and how it went.

Discover the thinker

TIME: 15 MINUTES

In this exercise, we're going to focus on meeting your mind.

I remember distinctly when I was first training in mindfulness meditation, there was an inner shift in which I became aware of my thinking and my mind. It was not like I hadn't had thoughts or been aware of them before, but in that moment, I became very aware of my mind and the thoughts running through it. I could begin to observe them and work with them. It was a bit startling initially, but very useful. That's what I mean by "discovering the thinker."

STEPS

1   Find a comfortable place to sit where you can focus undisturbed.

2   Sit with your spine fairly straight and your eyes open or closed, whichever is easiest.

3   Breathe normally, noticing where you find the breath, and then bring your attention to your breath at the nostrils.

4   Be aware of your breath and follow it as you breathe in and out.

5   Begin to be aware of and pay attention to your thinking. Notice the thoughts that you're having and the range of topics in their discursive, or meandering, nature.

6   Try to become aware of the thoughts and where they are coming from. If you can do this, then you will discover your mind. It may take several tries. Stay with this step, as you hopefully find your thoughts and your mind. If not, you can come back to it again later.

7   Sit for a while more and let everything go. Simply be aware of the breath at the nostrils, sit for a while more, and then take a few moments to slowly transition out of meditation.

Observe non-judgmentally

TIME: 20 TO 30 MINUTES

We are learning important basics, like how to sit, keep our back straight but relaxed, be aware of our breath and focus it at the nose or nostrils, and begin to locate our mind and be aware of our thoughts. This next step follows logically from what we have just done in becoming aware of our mind and our thinking. We are used to being carried along by random, discursive, and incessant thoughts—now we will take a step back and examine how our thoughts are often very critical and judgmental in nature.

STEPS

1 Find a comfortable place to sit, where you can focus undisturbed.

2 Sit with your spine straight, but relaxed, eyes open or closed.

3 Breathe normally, and then bring your attention to your breath at the nostrils.

4 Be aware of your breath and notice it as you breathe in and out.

5   Now, pay attention to your thinking. Notice your thoughts, the range of topics, and your thoughts' discursive nature.

6   Become aware of your thoughts and the judgments that are involved. Are the judgments about yourself, others, or both? What are the critical thoughts that you are having, and how do they make you feel?

7   Can you merely have your observations and thoughts without the judgments? Can you observe your thoughts and notice if they are critical, and if they are, pause and stop the criticism? Can you give yourself a bit of space, or step back (figuratively speaking), and merely observe things without judging? This is the goal. Try this several times, with short breaks in between. If you catch yourself judging, just note and drop it, and return to the meditation.

8   Sit for a while more while letting everything go. Simply be aware of the breath at the nostrils. Sit for a while more, and then slowly come out of meditation.

9   You may wish to make some ongoing notes, such as where and when the meditation occurred, how long it took, what breaks you took, and what you noticed as you did it.

Not too tight, not too loose

TIME: 20 MINUTES

The next step is a very important one in learning mindfulness meditation. We will be learning and practicing how to focus our mind, using the right amount of effort. Too much effort and we get a headache or are very tight; too loose and we lose our focus and drift off, or even fall asleep. This one took me a while to get the hang of. In fact, when I was learning, I used to get frequent headaches in my forehead. My meditation instructor used to praise me for my "strong effort," which was true. However, I wish she had pointed out to me that my focus was *too* strong, that I was overdoing it, and that was causing the headaches. I needed to ease up a bit. Much like the strings on a musical instrument, they should be "not too tight and not too loose." The proper amount of focus is a very important skill to learn in mindfulness meditation—we want the effort to be enough to keep us focused, but also relaxed and spacious for the best meditation experience. Please don't get discouraged if you don't have immediate success, as we will continue working on this.

STEPS

1   Find a quiet place to sit, where you can focus undisturbed.

2   Sit with your spine fairly straight and relaxed, and your eyes open or closed.

3   Breathe normally, begin to settle down, and bring your attention to your breath at the nostrils.

4   Notice and follow your breath as you breathe in and out.

5   Notice how much effort is required for you to stay focused on your breathing. Are you easily distracted? Do you find your mind constantly wandering off? If so, try to increase your effort and tighten your focus. Keep doing this as you begin to settle and stabilize your mind.

6   Once you have stabilized your attention, stay with that, while still focusing on the breath throughout the exercise. You can then back off the strong focus a bit and increase the ease of your focus. Keep working with this intersection of effort and ease of focus and attention. The ideal is to have stable focus and spacious ease at the same time. You may alternate this exercise with short breaks.

7   Finally, let all of this go, simply come back to the breath for a short while, and then conclude your practice session. Make notes if you wish.

The eyes: window into wisdom

TIME: 10 TO 20 MINUTES

Western mindfulness meditation is generally done with the eyes closed. One of the main reasons for this is that, especially when first starting out, students need to minimize their distractions, and closing the eyes is an excellent way to reduce external stimulation. The main downside to this is that students may also become sleepy, floaty, or drift off to sleep with the eyes shut. When the eyes are "half open or half shut," external distractions are reduced, but there is still some orientation to the outside world. With the eyes open, one tends to remain more alert and oriented, though there is more possibility for external distractions. From a higher meditation perspective, however, it is said in Vajrayana that the eyes are the door and access to the higher Wisdom, and that we should learn to meditate with our eyes open. I have personally found this to be the case, and it also definitely prevents one from dozing off. Additionally, with eyes open, one can more fully integrate the meditative state into all aspects of life.

1 Find a quiet place to sit, free from distractions. Using the same place in the beginning is often useful.

2 Sit with your spine straight but relaxed and eyes closed.

3 Breathe normally and settle in as you bring your attention to your breath at the nostrils.

4 Watch your breath, and notice it as you breathe in and out.

5 Do 5 minutes of meditation. Notice how you feel and any benefits or negative side effects of closing your eyes.

6 After 5 minutes, pause and rest for 1 minute, and then do 5 more minutes of meditation with your eyes half open. Pause and notice how you feel and any side effects.

7 Finally, sit with your eyes fully open for 5 minutes. As with the other two meditations, notice the benefits and difficulties, particularly in relation to the eyes being open.

8 You may wish to make some notes as to what you learned.

Redirect from distraction

TIME: 15 MINUTES

This will be the final meditation exercise in this basic series. It may sound like something we've already covered, and in some ways it is, but this exercise is a progression. You started out with all of the foundational steps, and slowly built up to this. This next step is really what you will be doing a lot of in mindfulness meditation. You sit, settle, find the breath, watch your thoughts, and now you'll work with distractions. This last step is very important. You are working on settling, stabilizing, and training your mind, but at this point your thoughts are generally quite discursive, and it's easy to drift off. When you become aware that you are distracted, simply notice it and bring your attention gently but firmly back to the breath. This is what we will do, over and over. We will use this basic skill as we engage in various other exercises. Please follow these steps until you feel comfortable doing the meditation without them.

1   Find a quiet place to sit, where you can focus undisturbed.

2   Sit with your spine straight but relaxed.

3   Breathe normally, settle, and bring your attention to your breath at the nostrils.

4   Choose if your eyes are going to be closed, half open, or open. Sometimes students start with their eyes closed as they settle, then open them some as they continue to meditate.

5   Notice your breath as you breathe in and out. In the beginning, I suggest you first notice the breath at the nostrils. Eventually, you may also wish to notice the breath elsewhere, such as the mouth, chest, or abdomen.

6   When you find that your attention has wandered and you get lost in discursive thoughts, bring your attention back to the breath. Try not to scold or get upset with yourself, as it's natural and to be expected.

7   Continue with this exercise in the same manner for up to 15 minutes if possible.

8   At the end, just sit and settle or rest for a short while, and then conclude. You may wish to make some notes and congratulate yourself. If you had any doubts before, you are definitely meditating now.

"In meditation leave your front door and back door open. Let thoughts come and go. Just don't serve them tea."
—*Shunyru* Suzuki Roshi

Seven-point posture of Vairochana: the gold standard

This exercise is the first set of instructions for the next step in meditation. It is suggested that you stay with the most basic meditation instructions until you feel ready to add this to your practice. In this exercise you will learn the seven-point posture of Vairochana, the "gold standard" for meditation posture. It comes out of the Vajrayana vehicle (page 2) and will make your mindfulness stronger and clearer, and hence more effective in working with anxiety.

STEPS

1   Sit comfortably, with legs gently folded if seated on the floor, or feet on the ground if sitting in a chair. Place your hands palms down on your knees, or alternately in your lap with palms facing up and left hand under the right hand.

2   Your spine should be straight; picture it as an arrow or a stack of gold coins.

3   Shoulders should be back and chest slightly open as though spread like a vulture's wings.

4   Your head should be erect and neck straight, the chin slightly lowered.

5   Mouth should be slightly open, as if to say, "Ahhhh," and the tip of the tongue should be on the palate behind the front teeth. Breath should be silent and natural.

6   Eyes should be open, or half open, gazing slightly down and looking anywhere from the tip of your nose to three feet in front of you.

7   Practice this posture for 10 minutes, then make some notes as to how it was for you and the effect on your meditation.

Head up, head down: a time for each

TIME: 10 TO 15 MINUTES

In the next level of basic meditation, two items become much more important: the eyes and the tilt of the head. We will explore both of these now. In an earlier exercise, we touched on the issue of the eyes closed, half open, or open, and the case for each of them. In intermediate meditation, it is somewhat assumed that the eyes will be either partially or fully open. Whichever you choose is up to you, and you may wish to experiment with both. Regarding the position of the head, it depends on how you feel. If you are having a difficult time settling, and your mind is particularly wild or discursive, it is recommended to bring the head and gaze down, to calm, settle, and focus your mindfulness. If you are feeling drowsy, dull, or lethargic, it is recommended to sit up straight with the head with the gaze up, and take a few strong, deep breaths to rouse and alert yourself. You will be working with the gaze up in this meditation.

1 Try sitting in the Vairochana posture (page 30).

2 Find your breath, begin to follow it, and settle.

3 If you are feeling sleepy or lethargic, sit up particularly straight, with your head up or slightly back, eyes wide open, and take a few strong breaths. Once you are feeling more alert, settle, and begin the rest of the meditation. If you get sleepy or lethargic during the rest of the meditation, you may repeat this step.

4 Start out for 30 seconds to 2 minutes with your eyes closed, and then open them halfway. Sit like this, following the breath at the nostrils, for at least 5 minutes or a little longer.

5 Next, pause and rest, no longer than a couple of minutes, and prepare to sit again.

6 Begin sitting as before, but with eyes open. The idea is not to be looking at things, but more just gazing into the space slightly in front of your face. While doing this, meditate following the breath at the nostrils, bringing your attention back to your breath if you notice yourself distracted.

7 In the end, sit for 30 seconds to 2 minutes, and complete the meditation. You may wish to make some notes.

Learning open awareness

TIME: 20 TO 30 MINUTES

This next exercise is my favorite, and it's the type of meditation that I most often use in my practice. You will do everything as in the previous exercises, but here you'll have your eyes open and gaze first at the floor, then the wall, and finally the sky. Obviously, this is a more relaxed and open meditation, but it also requires that your mind be stable and able to maintain focus.

STEPS

1 Find a comfortable place to sit without distractions.

2 Assume the Vairochana posture (page 30).

3 Find your breath; begin to follow it and settle.

4 Begin by gazing at an open spot on the floor. If or when you notice your mind wandering, gently but firmly return it to the breath and the open focus on the empty floor. Continue this meditation for 5 to 10 minutes, and then pause for a short break, about 1 minute.

5   Settle and begin again, this time with your head more upright and
     gazing at an open space on the wall. Follow the breath as you did
     before, turning your attention to it when it wanders. Try to find the
     balance between focus that is too tight and too loose (see exercise on
     page 24). Continue this meditation for 5 to 10 minutes and then take a
     short 1- to 2-minute break.

6   Settle quickly and resume the meditation, this time with the head
     more up, eyes open, and gazing at the open sky. Initially, pay attention
     to the breath and follow it, but at some point, you may wish to just
     be more aware of the open spaciousness. Do this meditation for 5 to
     10 minutes, then sit quietly with your eyes closed for a short while.

7   You may wish to make some notes regarding your experience.

Resting in the open awareness

TIME: 15 TO 25 MINUTES

You started off by cultivating mindfulness meditation that has a strong focus—this is essential. You want to also develop a spacious, relaxed, or more open quality, like the open sky. But to use openness or spaciousness, you first need to discover the openness, which you did in the previous exercise by lifting your gaze to the sky. Discovering the openness is very different than resting in it, just as losing weight is different than keeping it off. Ultimately, you want to be able to rest in this openness—this is what you will be practicing here.

In combating anxiety, the ability to find and rest in the openness is probably the single most powerful thing you can do, and that is why it's important to cultivate both stages—finding the openness, then resting in it. I've had so many clients sit across from me in the office, quite anxious and lost in their upsetting thoughts, who developed the capacity to just relax and drop the worry once they were able to access and remain in the open state.

STEPS

1 Find a comfortable place to sit without distractions.

2 Choose a posture that is fairly erect but relaxed.

3 Settle and find the breath, follow it, and allow yourself to relax.

4 You may wish to begin with your eyes closed, but fairly quickly open them at least halfway or fully.

5 Gaze at the empty floor, empty wall space, or open sky, and allow your open focus to settle and stabilize. At some point things may begin to relax and settle, or open.

6 If you find that things begin to open or clear and settle, see if you can just rest and remain in this state. You'll have fewer thoughts and much more ease.

7 If you find yourself in this open state, you may wish to think about some of the things that were bothering you before, the things that cause anxiety, and see what the level of that is at this point. Usually the anxiety has decreased significantly. You want to learn to recognize and maintain this.

8 Remain here for as long as is comfortable, without putting forth too much effort.

9 When you feel finished, slowly stand and return to your day, and see if you can take a bit of this peaceful and open quality with you.

Rumination and the mind, the heart, and the body center

TIME: 10 TO 20 MINUTES

Rumination is quite common, and it goes hand in hand with anxiety and worry. We have three levels on which anxiety and other psychological issues can be analyzed: thoughts, which come from the mind center and the head; emotions, which come out of the heart center in the chest; and sensations, which arise out of the body center of the lower abdomen, but can happen anywhere in the body. Rumination is the mind trying to understand and solve things when really, it's necessary to become mindfully aware of what emotions and physical sensations are occurring that are related to these thoughts and anxiety. Ruminating and trying to solve stress and worry in the mind will never work. You need to get to the underlying experiences, emotional and physical, that are driving the ruminative thoughts.

1 When you become aware that you are ruminating, turning things over and over in your mind, it can be a flag that you are stuck in your thoughts and are avoiding an underlying experience. You have not solved it with your incessant thinking and you won't be able to.

2 Pause, take a breath, and settle for a couple of minutes.

3 Shift your attention to your emotional center, and ask yourself what is the primary emotion that goes with this thinking. The emotion can be anything and does not have to be strong. Even a little emotion is fine.

4 Breathe with the emotion and let yourself feel it, without getting lost in it and without judgment if you can. Stay with this for a minute or two and notice if there is any change to the emotion.

5 Next, ask yourself what body area or sensation goes along with the thinking and emotion, then let yourself focus on the area and sensation, directing the breath into and through it if possible. Do this for a minute or several, and notice if there is any change to the sensation.

6 Be aware that we do this exercise, shifting from obsessive thinking to awareness of emotion and sensation, as rumination is the unconscious urge to avoid experiences that need work. Review the ruminative thinking and experiences that went along with it, and how to shift from stuck thinking to awareness of the experiences underlying it.

7 Notice if becoming aware of the underlying experiences allows the emotion or sensations to begin to shift, and for the incessant thinking to slow or even stop.

8 At the end, sit quietly for a minute or two and rest in meditation. You may wish to make notes before you return to your day.

9 This is a very important exercise, and one I suggest you master.

Find insight in the experience

When working with issues and the resulting anxiety, it is common to want to know what it's about. This is similar to rumination but differs in that it is more looking for insight and information than just letting your mind spin. The secret is to ask yourself the mental question, but then inquire into the experience that goes along with it, instead of just continuing to try to come up with a rational answer. Focus on the experience instead.

STEPS

1   When you're struggling to come up with an answer or insight into something you're anxious or worried about, pause and take a breath.

2   Acknowledge what you are doing: pressuring yourself to come up with an answer for something with no success.

3   Instead, pause and begin to breathe, as you have learned, and allow your mind to settle a bit.

4 Next, notice what experience—emotional, physical, or both—stands out the most. Begin to focus on that, letting go of the mental struggle to come up with an answer.

5 Continue to be aware of the experience that you identified, and breathe into or through that.

6 As you do this, you will likely notice some relaxation and some change or a shift happening in regard to that experience. With a little time, it may shift significantly or entirely dissolve.

7 As this relaxation happens, notice that the actual insight you were seeking will naturally and easily come into your mind.

8 You may wish to make some notes, then slowly breathe for a short while and return to your day.

"Nothing in the world can bother you as much as your own mind, I tell you. In fact, others seem to be bothering you, but it is not others. It is your own mind."
—Dalai Lama

When the past haunts us

TIME: 20 TO 30 MINUTES

It's common to get upset about all sorts of things; things that people say or do, situations, how someone may look or sound, and a myriad of other things. What we often don't know is that many—if not most—of the things that upset us are tied to issues from our past. We've all had many distressing moments and events throughout our lives, and we were unable to deal with them emotionally and find a resolution at the time. This could be for many reasons, including we were too young, it was too intense, it went on for too long, we didn't have the skills or support, and so on. The result is that these incomplete negative emotional experiences were then stored in our bodies and minds. It's important to resolve the old, incomplete or unresolved experiences of yesterday in order to move forward.

1   Find a comfortable place to sit, settle yourself, find the breath at the nostrils, and begin to follow it.

2   Think about the thing that has been bothering you, and allow yourself to recount it and fill in the details.

3   Notice how it makes you feel, emotionally and physically, and breathe a bit with it.

4   Now, ask yourself, "What does this experience remind me of?" Allow yourself to think back in time and see if you can recall earlier, similar experiences. Let yourself do this for a while.

5   When you think of one, or some, experiences and situations that this reminds you of, make a mental note of this. You may also want to write it down later.

6   Recall the old, past experiences that are similar to your current upset, and allow yourself to breathe with a relaxed jaw. See if you can get some relaxation, or even some shifting, in the intensity and level of upset associated with these past experiences.

7   Do you notice that your upset with the current situation or person is related to something unresolved in your past? Perhaps it is really the old, unresolved issues that created the sensitivity and upset over the current situation.

8   Observe if understanding this helps lessen your negative feelings and anxiety regarding your current situation.

9   When you're done, sit and breathe quietly for a short while, then make some notes and go about your day.

Plan ahead to reduce anxiety

TIME: 5 TO 20 MINUTES

If you think about it, you may realize that a lot of your anxiety is tied up in thoughts about the future; things you dread either happening or not happening, and it may also be related to painful events from the past. Since so much worry is directed at the future and negative things happening, one beneficial way to deal with anxiety is to plan for the future you want. You can do this meditation as a future planning exercise or when you're having anxious thoughts.

STEPS

1   Find a comfortable place where you won't be disturbed, settle in, and begin to follow your breath. Bring something to write with.

2   Think about and review the sorts of fears and worries that you have about your future. Notice if it's about your health, wealth, relationships, work, or something else.

3   Try to identify the main one or two things causing you the most worry about your future.

4 Notice the main worry thoughts and feel the fear regarding what you dread for the future. Allow yourself to breathe into and through the fearful emotion and any related sensations. Stay with this for a while, and see if it begins to relax and shift.

5 From this more settled and clearer place, think about how you would like your future to be. Think about what things you want to have happen instead of what you fear.

6 Lay out a plan as to how you can create the outcome that you want, instead of reacting to and avoiding the result that you fear. Later you may want to write this down.

7 What is an action step you can take right now towards realizing the future that you want? Visualize taking that step.

8 Recognize that you are either actively envisioning and creating the future that you want or fearing and worrying about that which you don't want. The choice is yours.

9 Sit for a moment, return to the easy breath, settle, come out of the meditation, and return to your daily life.

10 Build these review and action steps into your daily life, at least for a while.

Get comfortable with being uncomfortable

TIME: 15 MINUTES

No one likes being uncomfortable, and we all try to avoid it. We want what we want, and we avoid what we don't want. It's understandable but impossible. Life is full of discomfort, and so one great strategy is to become more comfortable, or accepting, of this discomfort. If we think of other areas of our life, such as exercise, over time, we can become more comfortable and accepting of the discomfort involved in training. The same is true of work, telling the truth, and other things that cause discomfort. We can't avoid all distress, but we can get more used to it.

STEPS

1 Find a place to meditate without distraction. Take time to find the breath, focus on it, and allow yourself to relax and settle in.

2 Think about things that make you uncomfortable and that you would like to avoid, and let yourself feel some of this discomfort. Become familiar with it.

3   Don't try to get rid of it; just be with it, as it is. This step is the key to this exercise.

4   Sit with the discomfort precisely as it is, no more or no less. Breathe with your mouth somewhat open, long and slow, with deeper and slower exhalations. Feel what it's like to be uncomfortable. Stay with this for a while.

5   Now, have a conversation with yourself. Remind yourself that "life involves discomfort, and that's just the way it is." Say this to yourself several times, and let it really sink in, the reality of it.

6   Go back to just feeling the discomfort, as it is, without resisting it. If you can, be accepting of it, or gently open to it. See if you can stay with the experience and not get into the mind commenting on it.

7   Notice if the discomfort, and your worry and anxiety about it, have lessened. This is a technique used for people with chronic pain and has been successful in reducing the need for pain medication.

8   Make any notes that you want or need to make, sit quietly for a moment while you notice the breath, and return to your daily activities.

How to make decisions

TIME: 10 TO 15 MINUTES

Have you ever been fearful about making decisions? I sure have, and sometimes it used to paralyze me. I was so afraid that I would make the wrong decision and something terrible would happen that I would get stuck, going back and forth, and get nothing done. It's a miserable feeling. The fear can be related to a lot of things, including failure, harm, striving for perfection, ridicule, loss, and so on. If we incorporate meditation in our daily life, however, we can work to prevent fear from paralyzing our decision-making abilities.

STEPS

1   This exercise can be worked with in the moment or in a "session with yourself" that you set aside time for. Either way, the process is very similar.

2   When fear or apprehension arises, take a moment to pause, pay attention to the breath, follow the breath, and begin to settle and reduce your anxiety level, at least a little bit.

3   Let yourself feel some of the fear, notice the body area that lights up with this, and breathe into or with it. Stay with this awhile, and the intensity of the anxiety should begin to decrease.

4   Now, you'll work with the mind. Ask yourself, "What is it that I fear will happen if I don't make the correct choice?" See what the answer is, and also notice the assumption that there is a correct choice.

5   There are often many options in regards to choices, or decisions that we have. Analysis can help you clearly go through the various options and probabilities regarding your decisions.

6   Also ask yourself, "Is this a life-or-death decision?" The answer is usually "no." You're back to wanting a particular outcome and to avoiding something else, but it's likely not life or death. Really try to understand and feel this.

7   Remember that many decisions are not final and can be altered at a later time.

8   Make your decision, feel however you feel, deeply and with acceptance, and move on. If you practice this, you can get good at it. Please remember that most decisions are not life or death, they're more just preferences, and no one has a crystal ball. It's about trusting yourself and your abilities to be decisive on your own behalf.

9   Sit for a little while; follow the breath; let as much of this clear from your mind, emotions, and body as you can; and get on with your day. You may wish to make notes. Congratulate yourself for making a decision.

Fear or anxiety: distinguish and extinguish

The distinction between fear and anxiety is an incredibly important one, but one that is often overlooked. Anxiety is usually thoughts about the past or the future; things that we did or did not like and that we hope will or won't happen in the future. These thoughts are disturbing and upsetting, can be disorienting, and can negatively affect our health and emotional well-being. But most important, these scary thoughts do not move us forward. Unless it's a conditioned response to a past traumatic situation, fear is an emotion related to something in the here and now. When I was scuba diving and got lost under the sunken bridge, I felt fear and knew that I could die. It was real, it was immediate, and I had to control my anxiety so that I could get out of the situation.

STEPS

1 Sit and settle, and focus on the breath. Continue with that for a while.

2 Think about something you are really anxious about. Let yourself go over it and into it, and see if you can conjure up some of the anxiety.

3 Once you been over it and the fear is rolling, just sit with the experience for a while and feel it.

4 Now, look and see if it's just anxiety or worry about what might happen that you do or don't want, or if there's an actual, immediate threat to fear. Sit with this a while and go over it. This is a critical distinction to make. Figure out which one it is.

5 If it's an immediate, real threat, then take care of it, right now.

6 If it's anxiety about what might or might not happen, make a mental note of that, and remind yourself that you are not in immediate danger. It's essential to understand and remember this.

7 Then, begin to think through a plan, which you can write down later, for how you're going to work with the outcome, whatever it may be. While things may be uncomfortable and not our preference, they are rarely disastrous, and we can adapt to all sorts of things. Remind yourself of this as you make the plan.

8 Return to your breath and follow it. Let go of the thinking and agitation around all this as much as possible. Return to your regular activities.

9 I definitely suggest that you make notes on this exercise. You can return to these notes and review what you discovered if or when the same anxieties arise in the future.

Mind full versus mindful?

TIME: 15 MINUTES

The title of this exercise is obviously a play on words, but it's also an accurate description of the two principal states of mind that you'll work with here. This simple exercise goes to the heart of why we learn and practice mindfulness meditation. Without mindfulness training, a typical state of mind is busy, discursive, and full of worrisome thoughts. The untrained mind is generally messy and unsettled. When we learn mindfulness, we begin to clean up our minds, focus our thinking, and settle our body and breathing. Mindfulness brings focus to the chaos, but this takes a while. Especially in the beginning, it's important to pay particular attention to your current state of mind and what's going on there.

STEPS

1 Find a place to sit where you won't be disturbed, and immediately turn your attention to what you are thinking. Don't try to control it; just observe it.

2   As you begin to see your thinking, start to do a little mindful breathing, focusing on the respiration at the nostrils.

3   Become aware of what your mind is doing. Notice what it's thinking. Notice if it is full of discursive thoughts, jumping from one to another. As the title alluded to, see if your mind is "full."

4   Now, settle into more full and complete mindfulness meditation. Sit quietly, focus on your respiration, follow the in and out of the breath, let yourself settle, and let your mind become quiet. Stay with this for at least 10 minutes.

5   Recheck your mind and your thinking. Notice the amount of mental busyness and discursive thinking going on now. It should be considerably less than before, and you may have a better understanding of the title, "mind full or mindful?"

Using affirmations to reduce anxiety and empower

TIME: 10 TO 25 MINUTES

Affirmations are usually thought of as positive statements we say to ourselves to achieve emotional or tangible goals. But, there's a lot more to it than that. The process of manifestation involves five stages:

1. Clarify what we want.

2. State it in the affirmative as though it has already happened.

3. Visualize it clearly.

4. Feel the emotion that goes with it.

5. Support it with ongoing action. The more that we affirm and manifest what we want, the more we reduce our anxieties. One of the affirmations can even be about being calm and confident, the opposite of fear.

1 Sit and mindfully meditate for 30 seconds to 2 minutes.

2 Think about some things that you would like to manifest. Typical desires often include health, happiness, success, prosperity, and so on. Take 2 to 3 minutes to do this.

3 Choose one to begin with, and slowly repeat it three times. For example, "I have excellent health."

4 As you repeat this, actively imagine yourself having excellent health and doing things as evidence. Notice the positive feeling that you get when you do this, and enjoy the atmosphere. Take 1 to 3 minutes to do this.

5 Proceed to another desire, and repeat the process. You may wish to limit it to four or five affirmations, at least to begin with. It is recommended to utilize no more than 10 different statements at a time; any more will dilute your focus.

6 When you finish with the affirmations, breathe mindfully for 2 to 3 minutes, and return to your day.

7 You may wish to make some notes. It is useful to keep a running tab of your affirmations and the results for those areas in your daily life.

8 Finally, consider the following: Affirmations do tend to work, and if you examine periods of worry and fear, we use precisely the same methodology, but in reverse. We are unknowingly working to create what we fear!

Challenge anxiety from illness or injury

TIME: 10 TO 25 MINUTES

No one likes to be ill or injured, and some people dislike it more than others. When we are sick or injured, it reminds us of our vulnerability, limitations, and our ultimate demise—of course it doesn't feel good! We are so used to being up and about and able to do what we want. Illness or injury interrupts this, making life harder and stirring up fears. The fears may be about aging, thoughts of futility that we may never recover, or even the wages that we are losing and can't afford to. Illness and injury can stir up a lot of fear and anxiety.

STEPS

1   The best time to do this exercise is when you are ill or injured. You will likely have more free time for the practice, too.

2   Find a comfortable place to do the exercise. In this case, you may wish to lie down, but please take care not to fall asleep. Do the usual beginning mindfulness meditation, finding the breath and following it for 2 to 3 minutes.

3   Take inventory of your illness or injury, and make mental notes regarding what you know about it and your emotional reaction to the situation. Do this for 1 to 3 minutes.

4   Be mindful of any worry or futile thoughts related to your illness or injury, and pay attention to the effect this has on your emotions. This is where much of the fear, anxiety, and suffering related to your illness or injury arise from. See if you can clearly understand this and the importance of managing it. Take several minutes for this.

5   Go back to the actual experience of illness or suffering and pay attention to it. The experience may be one of fatigue, pain, weakness, nausea, and so on—just be aware of the actual experience, and breathe mindfully into it. Do this for at least a couple of minutes.

6   The key here is to be mindfully aware of the actual physical experience, and separate that from the worry and futile thoughts, and then minimize the unpleasant emotions. Stay with this for another minute or two.

7   Often, we will find that our actual physical experience may not be that terribly unpleasant, and it's the worry thoughts and subsequent emotions that are so difficult. Spend another minute or so on this.

8   Mindfully breathe for 1 to 2 more minutes, and then let it all go. You may wish to make some notes regarding this.

> "Feelings come and go like clouds in a windy sky. Conscious breathing is my anchor."
> —Thich Nhat Hanh

PART TWO:
CALM *the*
BODY

Mindfully link diet and anxiety

In this exercise we will combine focused mindfulness with analytical thinking. We can incorporate meditation at meals, along with some mindfulness throughout the day. We need to become aware of the different effects that eating sweets and protein, and the resulting blood sugar levels, have on our emotional stability and anxiety. Blood sugar level has a significant effect on our anxiety. A blood sugar level that is too high or low can significantly increase our anxiety. Protein slowly raises our blood sugar level and keeps it steady for hours, while sugar quickly raises it too high, and then drops it quickly and precipitously.

Try this meditation in the morning before you eat. Think about what you usually eat during the day; especially how much quality protein you eat versus simple carbohydrates or simple sugars.

1   Begin the exercise by sitting quietly, settling, finding the breath, and following it.

2   Think about what you usually eat, and what your food preferences and aversions are.

3   In particular, notice if you are inclined towards a lot of sweets or refined carbohydrates.

4   Notice how much quality protein you usually consume, and whether it is spread throughout the day.

5   You can do this exercise several times during the day. Experiment a bit, seeing how you feel after eating more or less quality protein, and how you feel after eating more sweets. If you are inclined to sweets, notice if you get a spike in energy, perhaps too high, and then if you feel down or low after that. Note the emotional mood that goes along with this. Is there any correlation between your diet and anxiety level?

6   Sit for a short while at the end of each exercise, and keep good notes to make yourself more mindful of the diet-anxiety relationship in your daily life.

Balanced breathing: a quick anxiety fix

Have you ever been told, "Just breathe!"? Our emotions affect our breathing, and conversely, how we breathe alters our feelings. There are three fundamental difficult or challenging emotions that all humans have: anger, fear, and sadness. Each of these emotions has a distinct breathing pattern that goes with it. Fear, the primary emotion associated with anxiety, has the pattern of short and shallow inhalations, like a little gasp, and limited exhalation. Sometimes we may even hold our breath. The more we breathe like this, the more anxious we feel. We can calm our body and hence, our emotions, by altering our breathing. In this exercise, you are going to try balanced breathing with longer and slower exhalation. This is an excellent way to substantially and quickly reduce anxiety.

STEPS

1 This is an excellent exercise to do when feeling anxious. You can also practice it when you're not feeling so worried, so you will have some of the skills when a significant amount of anxiety does arise.

2 Find someplace where you can sit quietly. Though you can do it standing, I suggest sitting.

3 You may wish to gaze down at a blank spot on the floor or on the wall. Begin to find your breath and follow it.

4 Instead of merely becoming aware of the breath at the nostrils, notice how you are breathing, the amount of anxiety that you are feeling, and if your inhalation and exhalation are even.

5 Take charge of your breath and balance the inhalation. Inhale for a count of three or four, and then exhale for a count of three or four. This will likely require some concentration and forcing oneself to even out, or balance the breath. Do this for at least a couple of minutes.

6 Once you have begun to get some control over your breathing, and the inhale and exhale are even, add a more prolonged exhalation—at least a count of six, or even eight. Do this for several minutes.

7 By now you should notice a considerable shift in the ease of your breathing, as well as a significant calming and settling effect overall. Your body should be much calmer and more relaxed.

8 Stay with this exercise for at least another 5 minutes, if you have the time, and really let the relaxation and ease permeate your body and mind.

9 Remind yourself that you can return to this exercise at any time.

The complete breath: reduce anxiety, enliven, and balance

TIME: 10 TO 15 MINUTES

If you study activities such as yoga, qigong, or martial arts, you may be introduced to what is called the "complete breath." The thought is that we should breathe first into the lower abdomen, let it fill, and then allow the breath to continue up and into our chest, filling that last. On the exhalation, the process merely reverses itself, as we exhale first from the chest and then down to and finally from the lower abdomen. When we are anxious, as you may recall, we breathe mostly shallowly, and it comes from the upper chest. Complete breathing can really balance and enliven us, while substantially reducing our anxiety.

STEPS

1   Find a quiet place to sit. Sit with your back straight and not leaning against anything.

2   Find your breath, being mindful of the in and out, and allow your thoughts to settle.

3   Place one hand on your chest and the other hand on your lower abdomen. Pay attention to your breathing, and notice how your hands rise and fall, or not. Stay with this for a couple of minutes. Note how you feel.

4   Consciously shift your breathing to where your breath goes into your lower abdomen, and that hand rises and falls. Stay with this for at least a minute.

5   Next, start with the breath going into the lower abdomen, and that hand rising, and then let the inhalation and inspiration continue up into the chest, with that hand rising.

6   On the expiration, exhale from the chest area first, feeling that hand drop, and let the exhalation continue down and out from the lower abdomen, with that hand dropping.

7   Continue to practice this for at least 5 minutes. Hopefully, you will begin to get a smooth inhalation from the abdomen up into the chest, and then equally smooth exhalation from the chest down through the lower abdomen. See if you can get that rhythm going, and notice how you feel breathing like this.

8   Make plenty of notes about the process; what was easy or difficult, how long it took to smooth things out, and how you felt at the end.

9   Rise slowly, and return to your day, taking some of the ease and body awareness with you.

Using the mouth and jaw to relax

Through these exercises, you are systematically learning ways to work with your body, emotions, and mind, to relax and balance yourself and significantly reduce anxiety. This next exercise really helps release stress from the body, by teaching what to do with your mouth and jaw in breathing exercises. It's a simple but straightforward and essential exercise.

STEPS

1   Sit comfortably, back reasonably straight, and ideally sit slightly forward so your back is not resting on anything.

2   Your neck should be straight and neutral, with your head neither forward nor back.

3   Take a couple of minutes to breathe and become aware of your breath, and let yourself settle.

4   Let your jaw drop slightly, so your mouth is open one to two finger widths. Your mouth and jaw should still feel relaxed, not strained by trying to open too widely.

5   Sit like this and breathe for a few minutes, with the air going in and out through your nose and mouth, and get used to breathing with your mouth slightly open. You might want to focus your respiration at the chest, feeling the rising and falling.

6   Next, try going back and forth between breathing into the chest through the nostrils, and breathing into the chest with the mouth slightly open. See which one is easier and feels more open for breathing into the body. (I find mouth slightly open much looser and more relaxed.)

7   If your mouth gets dry, close it and move saliva around the inside of your mouth until it's moist again, and then let your jaw drop again and continue with the exercise.

8   If you've done any of the breathing into the body exercises before this, try using this open mouth breathing with those exercises. If not, just continue with this exercise.

9   See if your anxiety is decreased and if you are more at ease. Make notes and go about your day.

Body scan

TIME: 15 MINUTES

You are learning many of these exercises in order to reduce and overcome anxiety. Individually, they work to lessen anxiety and stress, and when you put them all together, which we will do at the end, they form a potent system for working with anxiety in any situation.

One skill we need is the ability to use mindful awareness to scan through our body and find where stress, anxiety, and psychological issues reside. S. N. Goenka was a famous mindfulness teacher whose entire mindfulness practice was based on body scanning.

STEPS

1 Find a place where you won't be disturbed, and sit comfortably with your back relatively straight. Ideally, your back should lean slightly forward, not resting on anything.

2 Become aware of your breath. Stay with this for at least a couple of minutes.

3   Starting at the top of your head, use your attention or awareness to slowly scan down your body. You may wish to make mental notes as to what this feels like.

4   Start the scan again, this time noticing what areas or sensations stand out. You may wish to make notes regarding this.

5   Start the scan again, and when you find an area that stands out or interests you, pause there, be aware of it, and mindfully breathe.

6   Continue with this for at least 3 to 5 minutes, and if your attention begins to wander, simply return your mindful awareness to the area that you selected in the body scan.

7   At the end, resume your attention to the breath and sit quietly for a minute or so. Make some notes at the end before you return to your day.

Breathe through it to dissolve it

TIME: 15 MINUTES

Sometimes clients wonder why they are instructed to focus on specific areas of the body. Most conventional psychotherapy focuses on an event or circumstances, and perhaps some feelings. This approach tends to be very thinking-oriented and overlooks the underlying experience. This is particularly true concerning the sensations that correspond to the story and emotions in the body. Up to now, you have been systematically learning how to scan the body to find areas and sensations that stand out, and determine the most effective ways to breathe. Now you will learn how to breathe into these areas, to clear the body of psychological events and issues and significantly reduce your anxiety.

STEPS

1 Find a place where you won't be disturbed, sit comfortably but pretty straight, find your breath at the nostrils, and begin to focus and settle.

2 Do a slow body scan, and notice what stands out the most.

3   Shift your attention from your breath at the nostrils, and pay attention to that body area.

4   Now, imagine that you can literally breathe into the body area that you're paying attention to. Breathe through the body, and right into and through that area. Stay with this for at least 3 to 5 minutes.

5   If the breath doesn't seem to want to go through the area, then imagine breathing around it. If this happens, it's not unusual that if you try again later, the breath will seem to go into and through the area of focus.

6   If the region of body tension begins to lessen, or even dissolve, that is fine, and actually desirable. It may also start in one area, shift, then move to another area. Continue to follow the place that stands out the most, and imagine breathing into and through it.

7   Please make some notes before returning to your day.

Mindful standing

TIME: 10 MINUTES

We stand a lot during our day, but rarely mindfully. Standing also takes some effort and can be a bit stressful and anxiety provoking. Since we stand often, it is a natural activity to use as the subject of mindfulness meditation. This meditation will continue with the theme of body, or somatic awareness, and being mindful of your physical experience and the effects it can have on you emotionally, mentally, and in reducing our anxiety.

STEPS

1 Sit for a minute or two, with your spine reasonably straight but relaxed, and focus your attention on your breath, as you settle physically and mentally.

2 When you've established a measure of mindful awareness, stand up, and just remain standing. Notice what your attention is drawn to and what sort of thoughts you have. Return to the meditation that you were doing before you stood up, but while standing.

3   Notice what it's like to simply stand. What are your thoughts and feelings about this? Do you feel anxious? If so, what sort of thoughts or memories do you have related to this? Is the anxiety associated with the effort of standing? Do you feel anxious because you stand out more, literally, and it's harder to hide? Are there other things about standing that make you uncomfortable or anxious? Please notice these and make some notes, at least mentally.

4   Using the Body scan (page 67), breathe into any areas that stand out.

5   Try to focus your careful attention on the body areas of interest and imagine breathing into or through these. Stay with this for at least 1 to 2 minutes.

6   Now, add to this awareness of your body and its alignment and balance. Are your feet evenly spaced at about shoulder width? Are you standing equally on your two feet, or do you tend to load one more than the other? Is your body fairly erect and shoulders comfortably back? Is your head balanced and straight on your shoulders? Are your shoulders relaxed, or hunched towards your ears? Whatever you discover, see if you can use awareness to adjust those things.

7   Return to just standing with awareness, and see if you can add a bit of Balanced breathing (page 61).

8   Make any useful notes, and return to your day.

> "If you are depressed, you are living in the past. If you're anxious, you are living in the future. If you are at peace, you are living in the present."
> —Lao Tzu

Center and balance to reduce anxiety

TIME: 5 TO 15 MINUTES

This mindfulness meditation explores the next step in becoming relaxed and comfortable in our body, more centered and grounded, more at ease, and with significantly less anxiety.

Being off balance and uncentered is particularly prevalent in the Western culture; when we stand and move, we tend to be off balance and not centered in our body. Consequently, we are ineffective in our movement and interactions, bear additional effort and strain, and carry an ungrounded, uncentered, and anxious feeling inside.

I've learned an enormous amount about balance centering during my decades of study in the martial arts and sports. Physically, it's one of the most valuable things I've learned, and it greatly affects my sense of well-being and reduces my anxiety level. I'm eager to share its benefits with you.

1 Start by just standing, paying attention to the balance and symmetry of your body, and breathing mindfully.

2 Now, shift your mindful attention to your lower abdomen, and begin to breathe in and out. This too is similar to a previous exercise (The complete breath, page 63), where you directed the respiration into the lower abdomen. Stay with this for a while, at least 2 to 3 minutes.

3 Next, allow your shoulders to drop and relax, and let your head sort of float on top of your shoulders. Do this for at least a minute.

4 Check your stance and ensure that your feet are about shoulder width apart, and continue to focus your respiration into and through your lower abdomen. Keep in mind that your lower abdomen is the center of your body and physical movement, and that is why we are focusing on it.

5 Make sure your knees are not locked, and there's a little flex and softness to them. Continue your mindful breathing into the lower abdomen, and be aware of your body and your posture. Stand this way for 3 to 5 minutes, noticing if your mind wanders and bringing it gently but firmly back to the exercise.

6 Imagine that roots are growing from your hands and bottoms of your feet down and into the earth, connecting you to the ground. You might prefer the imagery of water flowing, connecting you to the ground. Really let yourself settle. Try this for about a minute.

7 Continue with all of the above, standing in a centered and grounded manner, body relaxed and knees soft, directing your respiration into the lower abdomen, and feeling your connection through your hands and feet and into the ground.

8   Now, let your gaze be soft and relatively open as if you are gazing into the space in front of you, not sharply focused or fixated on any particular thing. Try this for another minute.

9   As you practice this meditation, use the help of a friend to give yourself a little test as to how you are doing. Stand in this centered posture, and have them stand in front of you. Slowly, not suddenly, they can very gently press on your chest to see how grounded or centered you are. If you're not very grounded, you will easily be pushed off balance to the rear, but if you are centered and grounded, you will be able to maintain your relaxation, strength, and stable position. The more anxiety and mental ruminations you have, the harder this exercise will be.

Mindful walking

In this mindfulness meditation, we will expand on the preceding exercise, though each exercise can stand alone and serve to reduce anxiety. As you develop your balance and center, as you stand and move, you can greatly enhance your sense of well-being, both physically and emotionally. When we are anxious, we are unbalanced and are centered too high up in our body. Think about it—tense shoulders, a tight jaw, a furrowed brow—these are some of the ways stress manifests in our upper body, making us vulnerable to stress, fear, and worry. Here you'll learn to stand and move in a centered and balanced manner; with it, you will have more energy, ease, calm, and presence.

STEPS

1   Begin by sitting in the mindfulness meditation posture and settle yourself. Review the steps from previous exercises if necessary.

2   Slowly stand and find a balanced and centered body posture. Shift your breath awareness to the lower abdomen, and breathe into the lower belly. Do this for at least a couple of minutes. Notice what happens to your stress level and your anxiety as you do this. It should decrease.

3   Check your body for relaxed shoulders, head floating lightly on top of the shoulders, eyes gazing ahead and not focused on anything, knees soft, and feet parallel and shoulder-width apart. Continue for 4 to 5 minutes.

4   Maintaining this balance and awareness, take a couple of steps and see if you can keep the balance, awareness, and ease. Repeat this several times, with a slight pause in between to re-center yourself.

5   Continue with the exercise and add one more thing; something that my aikido sensei suggests. As you stand, and particularly as you step and walk, imagine a bright light in your lower abdomen, which you must lead with to be able to see where you are going. This will help give you the lower abdominal awareness, and remind you that your movement and center should be directed from here. Continue the stepping and walking exercise for at least a few more minutes.

6   If you feel more confident, you might go outside for a walk, occasionally pausing to reconnect and re-center.

7   This is an excellent exercise to utilize when you go walking or hiking, and will significantly strengthen this awareness and skill, as well as greatly increase your calm and reduce anxiety.

Alter the day's course

TIME: 10 TO 15 MINUTES

We all know what it's like to "have a bad day." It may be one of those days that unpleasant things just keep happening, seemingly with no end. However, some people think of a bad day as one in which they just don't feel very good, regardless of what things happen to them. It might also be a combination of those two. The key is to differentiate our actual experience from what our negative mind talk is saying, and not let our negative thinking run away with us, spoiling everything in sight.

STEPS

1   Wherever you are, when you think you are "having a bad day," pause and find a place to do some mindfulness meditation. It doesn't have to be the ideal place, just a place where you can go to pause and focus for a while.

2   Find your breath, be aware of the in and out, and let yourself begin to settle, even if it's only a little bit. Take 2 to 3 minutes to do this.

3 What are the thoughts, emotions, and physical experiences that go along with your "bad day"? Think about this for a couple of minutes.

4 See if you can begin to separate the actual events and experiences from the thought, "I'm having a bad day." "Having a bad day" is merely a label you have placed on a series of experiences and a prediction of the future, none of which are positive or likely to be useful. Take a couple of minutes to do this.

5 You may separate the various events, noticing how you think and feel about each of them, and breathe into them, allowing 1 to 2 minutes for each one.

6 Keep in mind that whatever we tend to speak aloud, visualize, and have strong feelings about will be more likely to happen or to continue. You can halt the negative mental and verbal cascade, and then do things to turn the day around. Take a minute to contemplate this.

7 Consider what kinds of things you can change to alter the direction of your day. Take about 2 minutes to contemplate the changes you wish or need to make.

8 Be kind, gentle, and loving with yourself as you engage with this and alter the course of your day.

Rest trumps anxiety: a relaxation exercise

TIME: 10 TO 25 MINUTES

Following my abdominal surgery and in the ensuing months, I found that I had PTSD from all the traumatic experiences. This resulted in frequent anxiety attacks, often in the afternoon, and caused me enormous anxiety and distress. What I found enormously helpful was to take a break and lie down for a little while, using a meditative exercise to find the emotion and/or physical experience inside that goes with the thoughts and anxiety. To be able to lie and rest, take a break from responsibilities, and just focus on the experience of incredible anxiety can be very healing. In my experience, this would usually significantly lessen the anxiety or even dissolve it entirely. You need to be able to take a break, lie down, and rest in order to do this exercise. When anxiety is really starting to build, and nothing you've been doing is cutting through it, try this mindfulness meditation exercise.

1 Find a quiet place to lie down and rest, hopefully where you won't be disturbed.

2 Begin to feel the anxiety, realizing that with this type of exercise, it may be quite intense and pervasive. Don't try to avoid the fear or get away from it, but try not to get lost in or overwhelmed by it either. Begin to breathe mindfully.

3 This type of high anxiety often involves negative and even catastrophic thinking. Just notice and be aware of this, and keep returning your attention to your breath.

4 Shift your attention from your thinking to the emotion and especially the sensations, and then breathe into and through them.

5 Focus on the sensations, and imagine directing the breath into and through them. Try to let go of the frightening and discursive thoughts, returning to the sensations and the breath, over and over.

6 This meditation can take some time to master, as the anxiety level that generally accompanies it can be quite high, but with persistence and patience, the intense anxiety will usually slowly begin to soften and decrease.

7 With this exercise, we are generally not looking for full resolution and complete relief from the tension, but more a sufficient reduction in it so we can function on a more manageable level.

8 Stay with it as long as you can, and then go back to your day.

Progressive relaxation: tense and release

In psychology, there is a classic exercise called progressive relaxation. It basically uses mindfulness and deep breathing while tensing and releasing muscle groups to create deep relaxation. In many ways, and without knowing it, this may have been the first use of mindfulness-type awareness in psychology. You do this by first tensing certain muscle groups, and then letting them go or relaxing them. This allows you to isolate muscle groups, sense what they feel like when they are tense, and then contrast that to when they are relaxed.

STEPS

1 This exercise is generally done lying down and with eyes closed, but try not to fall asleep.

2 Breathe mindfully, and scan and become aware of your body. Do this for 1 to 3 minutes.

3   Now, as you inhale, tense and hold the muscles of your face and neck for 5 to 10 seconds, then on the exhalation release them and just let go. Feel the contrast in the sense of ease. Notice this for 30 seconds to 2 minutes.

4   Move down to the shoulders and arms and repeat the tension, release, and contrast.

5   Then move to your chest and upper back, repeating the exercise.

6   Move to the stomach and lower back, and repeat.

7   Move to the hips and pelvis.

8   Move to the upper legs.

9   Conclude with the lower legs and feet.

10 You can make this short, say less than 5 minutes, or extended to 25 or 30 minutes. Consider where you were holding the most tension, and if you were able to relax. Then lie quietly for a minute or two more, using mindful breathing. You may want to make notes.

Bring your center down to settle

TIME: 10 TO 20 MINUTES

This mindfulness meditation exercise is derived from Eastern practices, such as Taoism, Tibetan Buddhism, kung fu, qigong, and aikido. When we are anxious and unsettled, we lose our center and our connection to ourselves. Our inner energy rises, we become unbalanced, and it can be hard to settle and center ourselves. It's important to get this internal energy down. This exercise is designed to do precisely that, and it has been cultivated and refined over thousands of years. You can also do this as a quick exercise to settle yourself. It will only take a few minutes.

STEPS

1   You may do this exercise either sitting or standing, and it's best to practice this before anxiety strikes so that you will have some proficiency when it does.

2   Review The complete breath (page 63), where we practice breathing into the lower abdomen, then sit for a couple of minutes, and focus on breathing into the lower abdominal area. Get comfortable with this.

3   Next, while focusing your breath into the lower abdomen, pause after the inhalation and let the inspiration remain in the lower abdomen. Repeat this for 1 to 2 minutes.

4   Next, when you direct your breath into the lower abdomen and pause, imagine it being compressed there. Use the mental image of a French coffee press coming down through the body and squeezing the breath in this area. Practice visualizing this for a minute or two while you breathe.

5   Continue to breathe into the lower abdomen, hold the inspiration there, compress the breath there, and hold it for a little while, then exhale and start over. Try to stay relaxed as you do this and don't strain in the compressing and holding steps.

6   Make note of the effect this has on your overall feeling and anxiety in particular.

"Stop, breathe, look around and embrace the miracle of each day, the miracle of life."
—Jeffery A. White

Calm sexual anxieties

TIME: 15 MINUTES

It's not uncommon to have anxiety around sexual issues, which can come from a myriad of sources. These include, but are not limited to, early abuse or molestation, sexual assault, religious taboos, feeling pressured or manipulated, lack of experience, body image, hypo- or hypersexual urges, gender preference confusion, and others. I encourage you to provide yourself with a lot of self-acceptance, love, compassion, understanding, and encouragement in this area. Mindfulness meditation tools can help you work with your sexual anxieties. This is another area in which it's often useful to do some work on it by yourself before the worries arise in a sexual situation. Steps 1 through 5 will show you how to practice, and steps 6 through 9 will explore how this can be done in the moment with a supportive partner.

1   I recommend working on this by yourself before you are faced with it in a live situation. You may wish to start by making a list of the sexual triggers, memories, uncertainties, and activities that cause you sexual anxiety. As you practice, you may want to start with things that cause less stress, work with them, and then build up to the ones that produce more anxiety.

2   Sit in a comfortable meditative posture, focus the attention on the breath, and settle. Think of an element that you would like to work with, find a bit of the emotion that goes with the thoughts and story, and locate the body sensations associated with it. Now, open the mouth slightly, and direct the respiration into and through the sensations, mostly letting the thoughts and story go. Continue with this as the sensations begin to relax and eventually shift.

3   Mentally, give yourself self-acceptance and praise, and send yourself lots of love and warmth. After working with the actual emotional and physical experiences, it can be useful to work with it cognitively, such as telling yourself positive things.

4   You can continue with this sequence and go through the entire list over time, gradually reducing your anxiety while building your ease and confidence. It does take some work and persistence, but it is definitely worth it.

5   At the end of each session, give yourself some praise and encouragement, sit in regular mindful meditation for a minute or two, make some notes, and then return to your day.

6   Now let's consider a situation involving another person. When you are in a sexual situation, you'll want to be especially mindful, moment by moment, of what you are experiencing mentally, emotionally, and physically. Stay connected with yourself, and go at a pace that allows you to do that.

7   Focus on the physical sensations and how you are feeling emotionally. Breathe in a balanced way with a longer and slower exhalation. Try to go slowly enough to stay connected in this way.

8   First, feel the connection with yourself, and maintain the connection with the other person. Stay aware of your breathing, keep it calm and slower, feel your body, notice the emotion, be mindful of the other person and your feelings towards them, and proceed mindfully.

9   If anything happens to trigger you, pause and try to communicate this to your partner. Return to balanced breathing with the long, slow exhalation, feeling the sensations and breathing into them, and not getting lost in the emotion or the thoughts. You may need to stop, and then resume the activity at a later time. It is vital to have a supportive partner who will work with you.

Healing your relationship with food

Is your relationship with food and eating fraught with anxiety, confusion, self-judging, and sometimes self-loathing? If so, this is challenging, since cooking and eating are things that we must do every day just to survive. Food can be a source of enjoyment; however, rare is the person who has no emotional baggage around what they eat, how much they eat, and their size and weight. Many factors can confound this necessary activity. These include such things as being bottle or breast-fed, being hurried, being forced to "clean the plate," eating for consolation, the body type we were born with—the list goes on. Please be very loving, understanding, compassionate, and encouraging towards yourself as you work through this meditation.

1 You can do this exercise alone or with others when you're about to eat, thinking about eating, or recalling a memorable incident with food and eating.

2 Begin sitting comfortably, breathing in a balanced manner, and mindfully focusing on your breath at the nostrils. Let yourself settle, then begin to think about food and eating.

3 Notice what thoughts, memories, or associations come to mind. Move now to the emotional level, and notice what feelings you have. Mindfully focus on the feelings, and be aware of it just as it is. Stay with it a minute or two.

4 Move your attention to the physical level, and breathe into your body, noticing sensations associated with this, and direct the breath into and through these areas.

5 See if there are memories, emotions, or sensations that would not be typically associated with appetite and satiation. Pay particular attention to these; you may wish to make some notes, either now or later.

6 Attempt to eat mindfully as described in the Mindful eating exercise (page 171). Notice any feelings that might make you want to eat hurriedly, excessively, or compulsively. This can also work in reverse, such as with anorexia. Just stay with the awareness of the act of eating, along with any confounding mental or emotional risings.

7 Whatever comes up, try just to notice it with an open, loving, and accepting attitude. Remind yourself that the purpose of eating is to provide enjoyment and nourishment.

8 Make some notes on this exercise, then return to the Basic mindfulness meditation (page 18) for a bit, before getting back to your day.

Balance yourself

TIME: 5 TO 25 MINUTES

Balance is something that we usually take for granted, unless we have had a fall, or when we get older. I worked as a psychologist in senior care centers for 19 years, and witnessed an enormous amount of anxiety around falling. They were so scared of "going down," and they knew how serious it could be. If we don't have steady balance, simple things can seem quite challenging, and going certain places can feel treacherous. Balance is an excellent area to use mindfulness to minimize anxiety. You can do this exercise alone or when you're standing with friends, in a meeting, or in line. My favorite place to do this is the deli, while I wait to order.

STEPS

1   Sit quietly and meditate for a minute or two.

2   Take a minute to consider your own sense of balance. Have you stumbled or fallen, and if so, how do you feel about this? Keep breathing mindfully. Take another minute as you do this.

3   Stand up and find a place to practice your balance. If you are unsteady, you may want to be near a wall or sturdy chair that you can grab or hold on to.

4   While standing, raise one foot, mindfully breathing and feeling your body. See how long you can balance, without overdoing it. Repeat with the other side.

5   Continue to breathe mindfully and see how you feel. Is it more comfortable on one side than the other? Mentally make a note of this, as you maintain mindfulness. Resting when you need to, you can repeat this several times.

6   If you have a circular balance board or a balance cushion, you can up the game even higher. Repeat the above steps with these balance items, if you have them. Be sure to have something to hang onto if you need it.

7   Resume mindful breathing for 30 seconds to 2 minutes, and then continue your day.

Mindful stair use

Going up or down the stairs involves some risk, and for some people this activity involves a measure of anxiety. Such anxiety is especially prevalent when one is older, has balance issues, has a history of falling, is weak, or is not feeling well. This exercise also makes an excellent movement exercise to practice mindfulness while moving on flat ground.

STEPS

1   Find some stairs to practice on, and stand or sit while mindfully focusing on breathing for a couple of minutes.

2   Please use the railing, or at least have it immediately accessible. Falling down stairs is a common fear, but falling while going upstairs can also result in a "face plant" and wrist injury. You may wish to also review the exercise on mindful walking for some pointers.

3   Start at the bottom of the staircase. As you go up the stairs, step slowly and mindfully place your feet as you go. Focus on the inhalation as you go upstairs, so the breath can help pull you up the steps. Pause as needed as you go up, reflecting on how it feels.

4   At the top of the stairs, pause for a minute or two, and
    mindfully breathe.

5   Prepare and then proceed slowly down the stairs, grasping the railing
    and looking down in front of you. Focus on the exhalation as you go
    down, letting the respiration and downward step sink your weight
    into your lower body and feet. Don't bend over or lean forward as you
    descend. Take your time, and breathe mindfully.

6   Pause at the bottom, and breathe mindfully for a minute or two.

7   Repeat as often as you like or are able. Use this mindfulness anytime
    you are climbing or descending stairs.

Using mindfulness to relieve pain

TIME: 5 TO 25 MINUTES

We all know what pain feels like, and we all want to avoid it. This is particularly true if it's a chronic pain or if it's severe. Pain can really wear you down, make you tired, ruin your motivation, increase depression and anxiety, and make life seem futile. Alternative treatments are constantly being sought to help in the management of chronic pain. Mindfulness meditation has a lot to offer in the area of pain reduction, as shown by numerous studies that indicate moderate pain reduction through the use of mindfulness. At least one way this occurs is by blocking non-opioid pain receptors in the brain. Another mechanism involves relaxation of tissues surrounding the pain site, thus reducing secondary pain aggravation.

STEPS

1   Stand, sit, or lie down to do this exercise. Spend 30 seconds to 2 minutes mindfully breathing and getting into a meditative state.

2 Notice where the pain is, how severe, and if it is constant or intermittent. Take a minute or so to do this.

3 Direct the respiration into, around, or through the painful area. Do this for a few minutes, and see what the results are. If the pain is purely physiological and has no psychological component, which would be rare, then this would have no effect on it.

4 Though the pain may not completely subside, see if breathing in this manner will help improve it. This works by helping relax the area around the pain, decrease the negative thinking, and reduce the anticipation and avoidance of it. Continue with the breathing as long as you need to, at least 10 to 15 minutes.

5 Some people are visually inclined to imagine their pain as a symbol or drawing and see what happens to the image as a result of the meditation. Others achieve similar results by having an imagined conversation with it. You can use many modalities to do this.

6 Stay with that as long as you like it, and towards the end, shift your attention to just mindful breathing. Let things settle, and resume your day. You may wish to make some notes.

7 If you're having pain, especially if it is chronic, severe, and/or unexplained, you may wish to see a medical doctor.

Reduce dental visit anxiety

Most people dread going to the dentist, and some dread it more than others. When I was a child, I had a full-blown dental phobia, and once I even passed out in the dental chair. You can prepare beforehand, much like through the steps in the exercise on flying (page 177). Do what works for you. One solution is to stay present with the procedures and breathe into the sensations, but for others, it may be more helpful to use imagery of a favorite peaceful place and focus breathing there.

STEPS

1   While sitting in the waiting area, relax and do mindfulness meditation, focusing mainly on the more prolonged slower respiration, as well as feeling your hands and feet. This will help keep you grounded and in your body. You may wish to gaze at the floor, focusing on nothing in particular, as you breathe.

2   If sights or sounds are triggers for you, you may wish to close your eyes, or bring earplugs or earbuds and your favorite music. Do whatever you need to support yourself.

3   Try to stay aware of your hands and feet, and your slow, deep breathing. Try not to get caught in your head, imagining what the next steps are going to be and how you fear it unfolding.

4   Continue with body awareness and mindful breathing throughout the procedure, breathing into the sensations or focusing on imagery.

5   It is okay to ask the dentist to stop from time to time to give yourself a chance to reconnect and resettle. In fact, it's good to discuss all of this with the dentist beforehand so they know what you are working with.

6   When they are finished, you may wish to sit quietly in the waiting room or outside for at least 1 to 3 minutes as you meditate mindfully and collect yourself.

Facing death with grace

TIME: 10 TO 30 MINUTES

No one likes to think about dying, yet it is something that we will all do, and most of us fear, whether for ourselves, our loved ones, or both. This exercise is intended to introduce us to begin facing death with some degree of grace. It is not meant to be sad or negative, just matter of fact. We see the cycles of coming and going around us all the time. There is day and night, the start of the workday and end, the seasons, and even entering a room and later leaving it. It's omnipresent and entirely natural. Death can scare us when we consider the possibility of our existence coming to an end. Everyone will eventually die. Whenever it is, it is good to be prepared, and it's also good to not spend life being anxious about it. Mindful meditation can help with both.

STEPS

1   Find a comfortable place, where you won't be disturbed, and sit with the back straight but relaxed. Find your breath and follow it, as you calm and settle. Take 2 to 3 minutes to do this.

2   Begin to think about something that represents the cycle of coming and going: the seasons, day and night, youth and old age, and so on. Notice any thoughts or feelings that arise. Take several minutes to do this.

3   Contemplate what sorts of things you really enjoy about life, what your attachments are, and what it would be like to be without those. Take 2 to 3 minutes for this.

4   Keep going back to your breathing, and awareness of thoughts, emotions, and body sensations.

5   Now, remind yourself that someday you, this body and awareness, will be gone. Pause and see what that's like. Breathe with it for a couple of minutes. This is a critical piece of the exercise, as it's where we begin to confront our mortality. Be very gentle and loving with yourself. If you are a religious or spiritual person, this is an excellent place to call on that to support you.

6   Another crucial element of the activity comes next. Ask yourself, "What do I want or need to focus on in my life?" "What needs my attention?" "What do I not want to regret?" Take several minutes to do this. If it is a loved one's death that you fear, you can tailor these questions to them and what you want to do for them.

7   Sit for a little while, mindfully breathing, and then come out of the exercise. You may want to make some notes.

> "Living 24 hours with mindfulness is more worthwhile than living 100 years without it."
> —*The Buddha*

PART THREE:

CALM *the* EMOTIONS

Get close to anxious emotions to heal them

Especially here in the West, people are uncomfortable with their emotions, often men more than women. We typically have a very rational and cognitive approach to life, thinking that if we can name or explain something, then it is solved. Emotions, especially uncomfortable ones like anxiety, are avoided. But we must get to know our feelings and become more comfortable with them so we can work with them to transform and heal them. This mindfulness meditation exercise is designed to get us in touch with our emotions and reduce our anxiety.

STEPS

1   Find a comfortable place where you won't be disturbed. Sit with your back straight but relaxed.

2   Focus your attention on your breath at the nostrils, breathe evenly, and let everything relax and settle for 2 to 3 minutes.

3 Make a quick mental inventory of your most common challenging feelings. This may include fear, anxiety, sadness, anger, jealousy, envy, or others. Think broadly—we all have a wide range of unpleasant or challenging emotions.

4 Here we will focus on anxiety, but this exercise can be used with any emotions. Make a mental note of what types of situations tend to bring up anxiety for you.

5 Review at least one or two of these situations, and notice how thinking about it can stimulate the anxiety.

6 Just be aware of the feeling of dread; don't try to do anything with it. Specifically, don't try to suppress, avoid, or get rid of it.

7 Just let the anxiety be there, just like it is, and try to get acquainted with, or befriend it, as this exercise is designed to get us used to being in the presence of anxiety.

8 Congratulate yourself for sitting in the midst of your negative emotion. Usually just sitting with an emotion begins to lessen it. In other exercises, we will explore how to decrease it even more.

9 Take a moment to leave the exercise, and just return to mindful breathing for at least a minute or two.

Quiet the inner critic

TIME: 10 TO 20 MINUTES

We all have things that we don't like about ourselves. It may be because of the way that we look, our job, the amount of money that we have, comments we receive from others, or just the voice of our ongoing inner critic—the one that is never satisfied no matter what we do and is always criticizing and blaming us. Living with this sort of self-doubt is very unpleasant and the source of much suffering, unhappiness, and anxiety. In this exercise, we will begin working with this inner critic. Making a lasting change may take a concerted effort over time. You're worth it.

STEPS

1   Find a comfortable and quiet location free from distractions. Sit with your back straight but relaxed, begin to focus on your breathing, and settle.

2   Think about some of the things you don't like about yourself or that you have a hard time accepting. You may want to make a mental list of some of these, then select one to work with.

3   Review the trait that you feel the anxiety about. Just lightly review it, without getting into heavy self-criticism.

4   Begin to explore the emotional and physical anxiety and stress that goes along with this, while breathing into it, but see if you can do this more from an observing place with a bit of space and objectivity. Stay with this for at least 2 to 3 minutes.

5   Next, just mentally note to yourself, "It is what it is." Stay with this for at least a minute.

6   You can go back and forth between the mental noting and the breathing into the physical and emotional experience. Do this for another minute or two.

7   At the end of the exercise, see if you have a little bit more self-acceptance around this issue as well as less anxiety or stress.

8   Sit for a minute or two and just focus on your simple breathing at the nostrils, and then make some notes if you wish.

Forgive and forget

We have all done things that we regret. It can be challenging to face these things, and when we do, it may be difficult to forgive ourselves. These unresolved items can cause considerable rumination, self-criticism, and anxiety. This exercise will work at giving you the peace of self-forgiveness.

STEPS

1   Find a comfortable, quiet place. Sit comfortably with your back straight. Focus on your breath at the nostrils and settle into mindfulness meditation.

2   Think about something you have done for which you have a hard time forgiving yourself. It may have happened a long time ago, or it may be relatively recent. Notice if it was a one-time thing or if it is a pattern.

3   Review it clearly in your mind for a minute or so. Try just to observe it.

4   Notice the feelings or sensations that arise, and breathe into and through them. Do this for at least 2 to 3 minutes.

5   Say to yourself, silently or out loud, "I forgive myself for ___," and see what your reaction is. Do your mind, emotions, and body accept your statement, or is there resistance?

6   Whatever arises, use your mindfulness meditation skills to observe and simply be with the response. Do this for 3 to 4 minutes, repeating the forgiveness phrase as needed.

7   Try to allow the experience of forgiveness to permeate throughout the mind, emotion, and body. If you can, just rest in the peaceful sense of "forgiveness" and enjoy the new sense of ease and absence of anxiety.

8   If you are unable to access the feeling of self-forgiveness, then it may require another step, and we will cover that in the next exercise.

9   Make any notes, then rest in Basic mindfulness meditation (page 18) for a minute or two before resuming your day.

"The root of compassion is compassion for oneself."
—Pema Chödrön

Make amends for relief and closure

Sometimes we want to forgive ourselves or be forgiven by someone else, but it's just not working. There's something in the way, keeping things stuck, and preventing us from getting relief from this anxiety. This can be very frustrating.

If we look at the materials from the various 12-step groups such as Alcoholics Anonymous, we can find a handy tool in helping achieve forgiveness and release from anxiety. It's all about making amends—trying to repair things, or make them right.

STEPS

1 Find a comfortable, quiet place to sit with your back straight but relaxed. Become aware of your breathing at the nostrils while you settle into mindfulness meditation. Sit for at least 2 to 3 minutes.

2 Think about something that you would like to forgive yourself for, or be forgiven for, and review this for 1 to 2 minutes.

3 Think about what is in the way of the forgiveness and the lessening of the anxiety around this.

4 Come up with a plan to "make amends" in regard to this transgression. If the issue involves another person, it might involve writing an e-mail, making a call, or even meeting face to face. If the issue is within you, you might consider taking a course, reading a book, or continuing to meditate in the area you in which you wish to improve.

5 Now for the hard part; ask yourself if you will actually do this, and if so, determine the steps that you need to take, making a mental note of them.

6 Determine when you will begin taking these steps and resolve to do so.

7 Sit with all the emotions and physical sensations that have arisen while you breathe into and through your thoughts. Take several minutes to do this.

8 Return your focus to the breath at the nostrils for a minute or so before resuming your day.

Finding forgiveness

TIME: 10 TO 15 MINUTES

Sometimes we need to be forgiven, by others or ourselves, and other times we need to forgive someone else. Holding grudges can be a tremendous source of anxiety. In Eastern literature, there is a saying that goes something like, "Holding onto anger is like grasping a hot coal to throw at someone else, and you are the one who gets burned." This is just how it is when we hang onto our negative emotions, and it also causes us considerable anxiety as we ruminate about the situation. We need to learn to let go and forgive.

STEPS

1   Find your comfortable and quiet place, sit with your back relaxed but straight, and be aware of your breath at the nostrils. For 2 to 3 minutes, settle into your mindfulness meditation.

2   Think of someone you are upset with and have been unable to forgive and forget what they've done. Stay with this for about a minute. Notice the stress and anxiety, as well as other emotions, that you have been hanging onto.

3 Consider what your emotional cost has been because of this. Think about your feelings, such as how you likely avoid them and feel anxious if you think about them. Take 1 to 2 minutes to contemplate this.

4 Think about what the motivation for their action may have been. Notice your resulting emotions and the physical experience, and breathe into or through this for a few minutes.

5 See if the intensity of your emotions has begun to decrease and if you can have more of a sense of forgiveness for them. Take a minute to do this.

6 You may need to repeat this several times, combining the mindfulness meditation on the emotions and physical experience with the perceived reasons for their behavior. Over time, the level of upset should decline.

7 Return to the simple mindfulness meditation for a couple of minutes, merely following the respiration at the nostrils, before you resume your day.

8 Consider if you are ready to have a conversation or send that person a note. If not, you may wish to repeat this exercise.

Love yourself as you love others

TIME: 20 TO 30 MINUTES

To genuinely love oneself can be challenging. As humans, we are imperfect, and we know all the shameful things that we have done, the mere thought of which makes us quite uncomfortable and anxious.

In the 1970s, when the Dalai Lama first came to the West, he was told that Westerners often have a hard time loving themselves. He stopped and asked his translator to very carefully repeat in Tibetan what had just been said. Upon hearing again that it was often tough for Westerns to really love themselves, he just sat and sadly shook his head, as this was entirely unheard of where he came from.

One of the greatest loves is genuine self-love (not to be confused with narcissistic self-infatuation).

1   Find a quiet and comfortable location where you won't be disturbed. Sit with your back straight and relaxed, and focus your attention on your breath at the chest for at least 2 to 3 minutes.

2   Think about someone you really love. It could be a parent, a child, a friend, or even a pet. Really feel that deep love for them for a couple of minutes.

3   Now, imagine feeling that same deep love for yourself, and notice what happens. Are you able to feel that deep caring love for yourself, or does something else arise instead? Take a minute or two to consider this.

4   If you're able to feel that warm love for yourself, just rest in that for 3 to 5 minutes, and then conclude the exercise with a minute or two of mindful meditation.

5   If you're not able to feel that deep, caring love for yourself, sit mindfully and experience what that is like. What comes to mind instead of the warm, full love? You may feel emptiness or numbness, thoughts of your evil deeds, things that you don't like about yourself, or the realization that you aren't able to forgive yourself for something. Take 1 to 3 minutes for this.

6   Take a minute or two to examine your feelings and feel whatever emotions and physical sensations are there. Focus on your breath.

7   This is an exercise you can come back to over and over, as you work to dissolve whatever barriers you have to loving yourself and the discomfort and anxiety that accompanies that.

8   Sit for a couple of minutes in a simple mindfulness meditation, make a few notes, then go about your day.

Tonglen by yourself

TIME: 10 TO 15 MINUTES

Tonglen is a Tibetan term that means giving and taking. It is a seemingly simple mindfulness meditation but an essential and powerful one. On the inhalation you take into your heart, as a cloud of dark smoke, any difficulty or negativity from yourself or someone. On the exhalation, you imagine giving back to yourself or them, as light or love, the antidote needed for the negativity or whatever is needed for healing. We begin this exercise by providing it for ourselves, as we are all in need of healing, and it's usually easier to start with oneself.

STEPS

1 Find a comfortable place where you won't be disturbed, and sit comfortably with the spine straight but relaxed. Place your attention on the breath at the chest, and settle into mindfulness meditation for 2 to 3 minutes.

2 Once your Basic mindfulness meditation (page 18) has stabilized, imagine yourself standing in front of you.

3 Think about yourself and something you want or need. This may be something emotional such as forgiveness or love, or it may be health or relief from a physical condition such as an injury or an illness.

4 On the inhalation, imagine drawing into your heart area in your chest, like a dark smoky cloud, the negativity associated with this.

5 On the exhalation, imagine sending back to yourself, in the form of light and love, the emotional and/or physical healing that you desire.

6 Continue in the cycle of giving and receiving for at least 5 minutes if you can, and notice what comes up for you as you do this. See if some of the negativity begins to clear, and notice what your thoughts, emotions, and physical experiences are as you give this to yourself.

7 Sit quietly and settle, returning to the basic mindfulness meditation for a minute or two, before you make some notes and return to your day.

"As you breathe in, cherish yourself. As you breathe out, cherish all beings."
—Dalai Lama

Tonglen with another

TIME: 10 TO 15 MINUTES

The Dalai Lama said that this is one of the most important, yet simple exercises that we can do to benefit others (and to move towards enlightenment, should you wish). You can build up to doing this with people that you don't like. *Tonglen* is Tibetan for giving and receiving, and in the prior exercise, we practiced receiving from yourself the negativity associated with an injury or illness and giving back to yourself well-being and healing.

In this mindfulness meditation exercise, we will practice tonglen with someone else. Doing this exercise with someone else is more complicated and anxiety-provoking. There may be the fear of losing what we have or of catching an illness or negativity. Not only is this exercise useful for imparting healing and well-being to another, but it is also excellent for working on our fear and anxiety loss or harm.

1 Find a quiet and comfortable place, and sit with your spine straight but relaxed. Find your breath at the chest and take a couple of minutes to settle.

2 Think of somebody who is in need, either emotionally or physically, and imagine them in front of you.

3 On the inhalation, imagine their upset or illness as a dark cloud being drawn into your heart area, where it dissolves.

4 On the exhalation, imagine a warm golden or white light returning to them, giving them whatever it is that they might need: calm, love, well-being, healing, and so on.

5 Repeat this cycle for 5 to 10 minutes, noticing the satisfaction of helping someone in need. Also, find any fear or anxiety that you might have that you might lose something valuable or take on something negative or harmful through the exercise.

6 If anxious feelings arise, physically or emotionally, simply be aware of them and occasionally breathe into and through them, then return to "giving and receiving" with the person you're imagining in front of you.

7 This exercise is designed to benefit others, as well as get rid of any latent fears and anxiety that we have around our own losses.

8 Return to the simple mindfulness meditation for at least a couple of minutes before you make some notes and return to your day.

Reduce negative thinking to reduce anxiety

TIME: 10 TO 15 MINUTES

The way we think, positively or negatively, has a massive impact on our emotions, and by changing our negative thinking, we can allay our anxieties.

We are mentally talking to ourselves, whether we are conscious of it or not, almost all of the time. Unfortunately, we are often saying some very negative and scary things, with the result being an enormous amount of anxiety. It's time to change that.

STEPS

1   Find a quiet, comfortable place to sit, with back straight and relaxed. Find your breath at the nostrils and follow it for a couple of minutes as you settle.

2   Think of something that causes you a lot of anxiety. Go over the story around this thing, and as you do, begin to notice the thoughts that go along with it.

3   Pay particular attention to the negative thoughts, and how you feel when you have these thoughts. Take several minutes to do this.

4   Choose one or two of the main negative thoughts and examine them. Look and see if these cynical, anxiety-provoking thoughts are really accurate and supported by data. Do this for 1 to 2 minutes.

5   Notice what you found; most of our negative and anxiety-provoking thoughts have no immediate basis in reality. There is no one holding a gun to your head or about to run you over, and you are not dying this very moment. This is an important discovery to make. Take 1 to 2 minutes to examine this.

6   Feel the feelings that are behind all of these serious, scary thoughts. There are things that we are afraid of and that we have not dealt with emotionally. Now is the time to do that. Take 3 to 5 minutes, and breathe into the fear that is behind the scary thoughts. Feel a bit of the emotion, find the physical sensation that goes with it, and direct the breath into and through it.

7   Some underlying fears should begin to subside, though grave underlying concerns may need to be worked with in this way many times.

8   After some of the underlying fear has been lessened, go back, review the negative thoughts, and change them to something that is at least neutral, if not positive. Take a couple minutes to do this.

9   Return to the simple mindfulness meditation for at least a couple of minutes while you settle, make a few notes, and return to your day.

10 You can benefit from doing this exercise more than once for recurring issues or whenever negative self-talk arises. Do this as often as you need or like.

Find the settling magic of "the gap"

TIME: 10 TO 20 MINUTES

When learning and practicing mindfulness meditation, we must first learn to focus our attention and to stabilize it, and after that, we can learn to be a bit more relaxed and spacious. At times, we may have moments of little or no thought; sort of like a gap in our thinking, where the mind is quiet. This exercise deals with how to find that gap and prolong or expand it.

You will be working with your respiration, and the exhalation in particular, to calm your emotions and settle the mind. At the end of the expiration, there may be a gap of little or no thought, and you can simply prolong that.

STEPS

1 Find a quiet place, and sit comfortably with your spine straight but relaxed. Focus on breathing at the nose, and simply follow the breath as you relax, settle, stabilize your attention, and quiet your mind for 2 to 3 minutes.

2   Next, you'll balance your breathing, with a three- to four-count inhalation and three- to four-count exhalation. Do this for 1 to 2 minutes.

3   Now, keep the inhalation the same length, but stretch exhalation a bit longer, like a five or six count. Do this for 1 to 2 minutes.

4   Now for the fun part. At the end of the exhalation, notice there is a space, a quiet place, an emptiness, or a gap. See if you can rest in this "gap" and gently extend it. This is the crux of the meditation. Try to continue to breathe this way for at least 5 minutes.

5   If you get lost, or your mind wanders, gently but firmly bring yourself back to the breathing.

6   Try to be aware of the "gap," and what it's like to rest in or prolong that gap.

7   Go back to the regular balance breathing with a count of three to four on both the in and out, with awareness of it at the nostrils. Continue this for at least 1 to 2 minutes.

8   You may wish to make notes before you return to your day.

> "Flow with whatever may happen and let your mind be free: Stay centered by accepting whatever you are doing. This is the ultimate."
> —*Chuang Tzu*

PART FOUR:

MORNING

A wake-up meditation

TIME: VARIES FROM A FEW MINUTES TO 20 OR 30 MINUTES

This is one of my favorite meditation exercises and one that I do most mornings as I'm waking up.

Many people begin to wake up in the early morning, usually somewhere between 5 and 7 a.m., and have some time before they have to get up. There are often things on your mind, right? There are the things you have to do, forgot to do, don't want to do, or are generally worried about. These early-morning thoughts often carry a considerable amount of concern and anxiety. Sometimes you may even wake with a start and an intense fear with stress and worry flooding your mind, emotions, and body. This is an ideal time to do a "lying in bed waking up" meditation.

STEPS

1 When you're waking and in that state halfway between sleep and awake called hypnagogic, try to be aware of your thoughts, emotions, physical sensations, and what's on your mind.

2   Become aware of the effect your thoughts have on your emotions and physical sensations. Notice if the thoughts are disturbing and anxiety-provoking. You can readily train yourself to do this.

3   Now let the thoughts go, and simply focus on emotion and sensation. Then begin to breathe into and through the main experiences. Really try to stay with this, taking as long as you need. You want to get away from the thinking, and just focus on the experience and breath. The thoughts that go with this are usually quite scary, and we want to drop those, as much as we can.

4   Keep returning to mindful awareness of the sensations and some of the emotion, breathing into and through it.

5   You may find that you eventually doze off, waking up later feeling more relaxed and less anxious, and sometimes even all of the anxiety and distress is gone.

6   This is an excellent exercise to work with strong fears and anxieties, in the comfort of your own bed.

7   When it's time to get up, take a minute or two for mindful breathing before you get up for the day.

Get up when you don't want to

We've all had days when we just did not want to get up, and we would lay there in bed avoiding throwing the covers back and getting up. This can be due to lack of rest and being tired, but it is often due to anxiety and something that we wish to avoid. However, the longer we lie there putting off getting up, the harder it becomes and the higher our stress goes. This exercise is to help combat this.

STEPS

1   When you find yourself dreading getting up in the morning, this is the time to do this exercise. Make a mental note of this avoidance, and breathe mindfully for 30 seconds to 2 minutes.

2   Notice what it is you are avoiding, if it is something specific. It may be just anxiety and avoidance in general. Take 1 to 2 minutes to be aware of any thoughts, emotions, or sensations, and continue to breathe mindfully.

3   Prepare yourself to get up, regardless of how you feel or what's going on, and make it pretty immediate, so you don't keep lingering. Take 30 seconds to 1 minute to prepare.

4   When the moment comes, tell yourself something like, "Okay, get up, now!" Immediately throw the covers back and begin to rise. Do not hesitate.

5   Notice how good it feels to break through this and declare that you are now getting going. When feelings are anxious and avoiding, there is enormous relief in moving. Keep moving, as you feel what this is like, to get things into motion.

6   You may wish to find some easier things to do to continue your successful momentum, as you start your day. Congratulate yourself on getting going.

Mindful morning stretch

TIME: 5 TO 15 MINUTES

Many people like to do a bit of stretching when they first wake up in the morning. It can be done in bed, on the floor, or even while sitting on your cushion getting ready to meditate for a few minutes. A morning stretch is different than one that comes later in the day, perhaps tied to a yoga or workout routine, which is usually longer or more intense. This one is simply designed to help wake you up, loosen your body, get you more alert, and get you going on your day with increased calm and decreased anxiety.

STEPS

1 If you did the previous mindfulness meditation for waking up, you've already begun to focus your attention and become more present-oriented. This morning stretching routine will simply be an extension of that.

2 If not, take just a minute and allow your mind to become alert and settled by focusing on your breath.

3   You can make up your own stretches, or find a few easy yoga stretches online. You can also raise your shoulders and let them fall a few times, do gentle circles with your head, do arm circles, rotate your hips in both directions, gently and slowly bend forward towards the floor then come back up, lean back, do knee circles with your feet together, and do light calf stretching.

4   The key is to pay close attention and be very mindful of your movement as you are doing it, moment by moment.

5   Next, you'll coordinate your stretching with your breath. For example, you might inhale when stretching up or back, and exhale when strctching down.

6   The goal is to wake up and get loosened up, sharpen your attention, and coordinate your mind and body.

7   You may wish to end with a short standing mindfulness meditation, for 1 to 2 minutes.

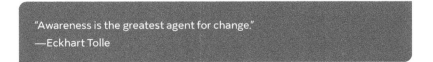

"Awareness is the greatest agent for change."
—Eckhart Tolle

Clear out the stagnation

TIME: 5 TO 10 MINUTES

This excellent exercise comes from Vajrayana Buddhism and fits very nicely into the morning routine. Advanced practitioners believe that during the night when we're sleeping, stagnant air and energy get stuck inside of us, and when we awaken, we tend to be groggy, out of sorts, and are often a bit anxious. This exercise is designed to clear out this stagnation and help get us going. It is generally done seated on the cushion on the floor, in a chair, or on the edge of the bed. For this exercise, it is vital that the upper body is a little straighter so you can get a good, full breath.

STEPS

1   Sit comfortably, but with your back and body a little straighter than usual so that you can take a full breath.

2   Sit with your head up and eyes wide open, looking out into the space in front of you.

3 Through the right nostril only, take in a full, deep breath, hold it for a moment, as you close your left nostril with your left index finger, then exhale once sharply through the right nostril. Repeat this three times.

4 Do the same thing on the other side, closing your right nostril with your right index finger, inhaling fully, and sharply exhaling through the left nostril, three times.

5 Breathe fully into both nostrils, then exhale sharply. Do this three times.

6 Then, with your mouth open wide, inhale fully as you draw your hands and arms out wide out to the sides and then back.

7 Through the mouth, exhale forcefully and fully, as you bring the arms and hands back to the body. Repeat steps 6 and 7 three times. It's not unusual to cough a bit as the stale, dirty air is exhaled.

8 In the end, sit quietly for a minute or so, to focus and settle your mind.

9 This can nicely lead into the next meditation, a short sitting practice for the morning, or it can be used anytime that you feel tired or sluggish.

A morning sitting practice

TIME: 5 TO 10 MINUTES

This is a straightforward and short sitting practice done first thing in the morning, and it doesn't have to be as lengthy or involved as the ones done later in the day. It's quite nice to start with the Mindful morning stretch (page 127), and/or Clear out the stagnation (page 129). If you are doing either or both of these other exercises, begin there and naturally move into this essential sitting practice. If you are simply doing the basic sitting practice, then simply ease right into it. Meditations like this start you off with a clear mind that is more likely to be peaceful and grounded and less likely to turn to anxious thoughts.

STEPS

1 Sit comfortably on the edge of your bed, or on your pillow with your back against the headboard, with the back reasonably straight and relaxed and eyes open.

2 You can also sit looking out the window, as you clear your mind for the coming day.

3 Breathe a little stronger as you work on focusing the mind and waking up.

4 Gazing out the window can be a useful visual tool to use with breathing to clear the mind. At some point, you may notice that your vision and clarity begin to sharpen, almost like something awakens, opens, and shifts.

5 Continue with this for 2 to 3 minutes more.

6 Bring your attention back to the breath at the nostrils for 30 seconds to 1 minute, and get up to greet the day.

Power breathing kickstart

We can feel anxious when our energy is on edge and rising up in our body, fueling the ruminating mind. We can also be nervous when we are sluggish and draggy and find it hard to get going and get things done. The latter is more likely the case in the morning, and doing some power breathing is a terrific antidote for this. The only caution is to not overdo it, as we don't want to become revved up and imbalanced. You can always add a little more of the power breathing should you feel the need.

STEPS

1   You may do this exercise either seated or standing. If you do it standing, be mindful and take care not to stumble or fall. For the purpose of this description, I will assume that you are seated.

2   Sit with your hands on your knees, your back reasonably straight, your head slightly up, and eyes open. Focus and settle your mind for 30 seconds to 2 minutes.

3   Your mouth should be open at least two or three finger widths, with jaws loose. If your jaws are too tight, just open them as widely as you comfortably can.

4   Begin breathing in and out, fully and deeply, with your mouth wide open. Some people find imagining the smile in the back of their throat helpful in getting things open. Others imagine making an "ah-ha" sound.

5   Try breathing this way for approximately 30 seconds. Monitor yourself carefully so you do not become dizzy, unstable, or fall over.

6   Pause and let yourself settle, noticing that you might feel a slight energy or buzz from it.

7   You can repeat this cycle several times, if you feel sufficiently stable and grounded as you do it. At the end of this, sit for 2 to 3 minutes before slowly getting up. You may wish to make some notes.

8   If at any time, you feel uncomfortable or unbalanced, return the breath to the usual style, and breathe slowly and deeply until back to normal.

"The practices of mindful walking, mindful sitting, and mindful breathing are our foundation. With our mindful breath and mindful steps, we can produce the energy of mindfulness and return to the awakened wisdom lying in each cell of our body. That energy will embrace us and heal us."
—Thich Nat Hanh

Finding what you want and how to get there

TIME: 5 TO 20 MINUTES

I've been doing executive and life coaching since the late 1980s, even before there was such a thing, and I have worked with many people, some of them award-winning, including managers, sales reps, therapists, entrepreneurs, CEOs, and lawyers. I have found that many people experience an enormous amount of anxiety around goals, intentions, and success, or lack thereof. They want to make a substantial contribution in life and do good work. The next several exercises come from the area of life coaching and are designed to help you discover what you want out of life and how to get there. Clarity, vision, and accomplishment are significant ways to move one's life forward and reduce anxiety.

STEPS

1   Find a comfortable place where you won't be disturbed, perhaps at a desk or work area, and be prepared to make notes.

2   Begin by focusing your attention on your breath, letting things settle, and allowing your thoughts to slow down and the body to relax. Become mindful.

3   Think back to when you were young and what you wanted to be. Stay aware of your breathing and your physical sensations while you review this. Notice why you wanted to be that, if that changed, and if so, why. Stay aware of your experience, thinking, emotions, and sensations, and breathe with all of this.

4   Notice how what you want to be has evolved over time, and let that desire come all the way forward to the present time. What do you want to be now, or what are your intentions in life? Continue to mindfully stay connected with your experience and breathe into, through, or with it. Try not to judge it, and simply be aware and accepting of it.

5   Notice if you have anxiety around all of this, and if so, why is that? Be aware, feel it, and let it go.

6   Notice any judging thoughts that you have around all of this. Using mindful awareness, let those go.

7   While continuing to use conscious awareness, come back to your goals, desires, and intentions, and decide if you're willing to stand behind those and make solid plans and steps forward. Notice thoughts, emotions, and sensations, and breathe into those.

8   Ask yourself, "What are the first one or two steps in this direction? Am I willing to take them?" Notice your experience around all of this and breathe into it.

9   Take one to two minutes to gently return to your awareness of the breath, calm yourself, and settle.

10 Make some notes before you resume your day. You can return to this exercise anytime to update or further it.

Accomplishing daily to-dos

TIME: 5 TO 15 MINUTES

In life coaching, there is a crucial area of focus called Getting Things Done, often referred to as GTD. With things we need to do in life, there is often an enormous amount of anxiety in getting started or following through. Luckily, there is a real science around GTD to help us accomplish this and reduce our stress. The key is to have one place where you write down everything that you need to do. Our goals inform our GTD list, and our GTD list advises our daily to-do list, containing those items we've chosen for the day. This exercise is about going over our to-do list and getting going.

STEPS

1   You may wish to do this meditation at your desk or work area. Get seated and relaxed, back relatively straight, find your breath, and follow it as you settle.

2   You may find it helpful to remind yourself what your purpose in life is and what main goals you are working on. Keep coming back to the mindful breathing and any reactions you might have.

3   You may need your eyes open for this next part, and if so, still return regularly to Basic mindfulness meditation (page 18) to keep yourself calm, centered, and focused.

4   Review your master list of things to do or your GTD list. Intersperse reviewing your list with mindful breathing.

5   Think about what items you have scheduled for the day, either looking at your calendar or going through it in your head. Return to the basic mindfulness meditation for 30 to 60 seconds, then compare your activity calendar with your GTD master list, and select the items that you will work on for the day. You may wish to write them down on your daily to-do list.

6   Pause and return to mindful awareness and breathing. Notice any anxiety reactions that you have to all of this, and breathe into or through these. Take a minute or two to return to essential mindfulness and settle.

7   If you are already dressed and ready for your day, choose your first item and get started on it. Otherwise, get up and ready for your day.

8   You can do this exercise every day.

Start your day with focus, not fuzz

When starting the day, it's easy to get distracted. There are some things that we should NOT do when starting our day. It is advised by the most productive people that we avoid looking at Facebook or other social media, checking our email, and reading or watching the news, for at least the first hour of our day. These waste a lot of time, make us lose our focus, and tend to make us anxious. Instead, we should do such things as stretching, meditating, planning our day, making our to-do list, and getting started on it.

STEPS

1   Plan the night before how you're going to start your next day, and then stick to it.

2   Upon awakening, get up and sit on the side of the bed, and take about 3 minutes to do a brief mindfulness meditation.

3   Then, notice any desire that you may have to check e-mail, log onto Facebook, or see the news. Mindfully feel what it's like to really want to do those things. Notice the thoughts, and especially the emotions and physical sensations, that go along with being drawn to those things. Mindfully breathe into and through them. See if you can overcome the pull and stay focused. Take 1 to 2 minutes to more formally meditate mindfully, feel the desire to engage in those things, and call forth your firm resolve to stay focused and not give in.

4   Choose the activities you will begin your day with instead, such as stretching, a more extended meditation, goal review and day planning, and so on. Do mindfulness meditation for another minute or so as you prepare to transition to one of those activities.

5   It is sometimes helpful to avoid having access to the Internet, social media, and news as we work on breaking this habit and significantly reducing our anxiety.

6   Without hesitation, move now into one of those productive activities, the ones that will lower your stress, increase your focus and calm, and enable you to get done what you really want and need to do.

A mindful breakfast meditation

TIME: 10 TO 25 MINUTES

Leading nutritionists say that breakfast is the most important meal of the day, and is correlated with energy, clarity, weight normalization, stable blood sugar, good health, and productivity. In the exercise Healing your relationship with food (page 89), we looked at reducing simple carbohydrates and getting adequate, high-quality protein. Another good strategy is to follow a diet low in saturated fat. These measures help keep the blood sugar steady, thus reducing anxiety. Another critical element is the reduction, or even avoidance, of stimulants such as caffeine. This is particularly true in regard to anxiety, as stimulants generate a lot of stress.

STEPS

1 This exercise is a combination of several other exercises. Part of learning mindfulness meditation is integrating different steps and skills, and finding ways to be mindful in various activities and moments throughout the day.

2 Sit at the table, and do your basic mindfulness meditation here. With your back straight but relaxed, pay attention to your breath and focus on the in and out breathing, at the nostrils or another place of choice. Allow yourself to settle, and be aware of where you are. Between each of the following steps, take at least a minute or two to do the Basic mindfulness meditation (page 18).

3 As you recall the exercise Mindfully linking diet and anxiety (page 59), plan out your meal.

4 Remember or read the practice on Mindful cooking (page 169). Prepare your food according to those steps.

5 As you prepare to eat, recall or review the exercise on Mindful eating (page 171).

6 With this part, be particularly aware, paying close attention as you take bites of food, chew thoroughly, swallow, then pause between bites.

7 Continue in this manner, throughout the entire meal, if you can. If you start to speed up, or your mind wanders, return to basic mindfulness meditation, focus on the breath, and resettle.

8 At the end of the meal, pause for 1 to 3 minutes of mindfulness meditation before you clear your dishes and go on with your day.

9 Note how much calmer and relaxed you feel.

"Anxiety happens when you think you have to figure out everything all at once. Breathe. You're strong. You got this. Take it day by day."
—Karen Salmansohn

PART FIVE:
EVENING

An effective evening wind-down

TIME: 5 TO 30 MINUTES

Anxious people often have a hard time winding down in the evening. Sometimes it feels like there is a motor running inside, or the mind just won't stop, and it can be challenging to let oneself wind down. In fact, winding down is a conscious process, and often involves several steps.

Don't have caffeine too late in the day (or at all) as this is often the leading cause of difficulty winding down. Avoid heavy exercise in the evening because the increased internal body heat makes it hard to slow down. Stimulating music, video games, and action TV shows can also make it difficult to relax.

STEPS

1   Find a quiet place where you won't be disturbed. Sit with your back relatively straight and relaxed and place your attention on your breathing. Sit and settle for 3 to 5 minutes.

2   Notice how you're feeling inside and if there is agitation or anxiety. If so, breathe into, through, or at least around it. Stay with this for a couple of minutes.

3   Consider fixing some herbal tea, something soothing and calming. Breathe and return to the meditation for a minute or two.

4   Think about what would settle your body and mind: a book, jazz or classical music, some light stretching, softer lower lighting, a warmer or cooler temperature, and so on. Continue focusing on the breathing and the meditation as you go through the possibilities.

5   Think of ways to avoid the blue light from digital screens. Is there anything you need to check before you put them away for the evening? Continue with your meditation and breathing.

6   Now put this plan into action. Continue meditating, as you have been, for another 3 to 5 minutes, then get up and mindfully follow the routine that you've mapped out for yourself.

7   Enjoy calmer and slower evenings as you learn how to wind down.

Nighttime settling without revving back up

TIME: 10 TO 20 MINUTES

This is a companion exercise to the previous one. Many people with anxiety have difficulty settling and relaxing. We spoke to this point in the previous exercise, but there is another element that frequently comes into play: cycling back up. With anxiety, there is often an internal motor, buzz, or mental chatter that can start back up quite quickly. To break the revving pattern, we need to be on the lookout and not give in to it.

STEPS

1   The best time to do this exercise is in the evening when you been working on "winding down," and through your mindful awareness you notice even a subtle inclination to "cycle back up."

2   When this happens, find a quiet place where you won't be disturbed, sit in the meditative posture, and follow your breath for a few minutes.

3   Become very aware of the effort you were putting into winding down, and notice whatever it is that was rising and encouraging you to cycle back up. This is important. Spend 1 to 3 minutes on this, as you continue your meditative focus and breathing.

4   Notice that there is a choice point that you've come to. You need and, hopefully, want to settle down for the evening. And, there's an urge or impetus of some sort to get you to speed back up. Sit with this mindfully, and notice the thoughts and feel the emotions and physical sensations that go with this urge to cycle back up.

5   Breathe into and through the inner experience that goes with the urge to speed back up. Take 3 to 5 minutes to do this. See if you can reverse the urge to speed back up, and return to the pattern of settling down.

6   Hopefully, by doing this, you have calmed the urgency and returned to the state of calm. Rest in this state for 1 to 3 minutes.

7   Congratulate yourself on catching this, and resume your evening, being mindful that the pattern may come up again.

The day in review

TIME: 5 TO 15 MINUTES

It's not unusual in the evening to be anxious with the mind spinning about all the events or unfinished business of the day. Psychologically, it can be useful to do a simple review of the day in the evening before sleep. It's pretty simple; you'll just go through the day, from morning until night, and notice what stands out the most. This exercise is meant to review the day's events, in order to let go of things. This can help reduce the mind chatter and anxiety from unresolved issues that linger from our day.

STEPS

1   Find a comfortable, quiet place where you won't be disturbed but won't fall asleep. Assume a somewhat more relaxed meditation posture. Begin to breathe and focus on your breath.

2   Think about what you did during the day. If you have difficulty recalling, you can consult your schedule and to-do list, then return to the meditative breathing. Take as much time as you need with this.

3   As you review your day, what comes to mind or stands out? What thoughts, emotions, and physical sensations do you have? Breathe into and through anything that stands out. Mindfully continue this until there is some sort of shift and relaxation. This could take just a couple of minutes or as long as 20 minutes.

4   See if enough has been reviewed and shifted to allow you to relax and prepare for sleep.

5   If so, this would be an excellent time to add a sleepy meditation (page 158), then enjoy a good night's rest.

> "It's a funny thing about life, once you begin to take note of the things you are grateful for, you begin to lose sight of the things that you lack."
> —Germany Kent

Reducing anxiety around wins and regrets

TIME: 5 TO 15 MINUTES

This meditation is quite separate from, yet related to, the previous exercise on reviewing the day. In this exercise, you'll focus specifically on what we call wins and regrets. We all have things that we are working on, positive habits we want to strengthen and negative ones we wish to eliminate. Our awareness of, efforts towards, and results with these things can all be anxiety-provoking, especially if we are not succeeding. This exercise is designed to assist you in this area and reduce your anxiety.

STEPS

1 Find a comfortable place where you won't be disturbed but won't fall asleep. Sit comfortably, but remain alert. Focus on your breathing, becoming mindful and letting your mind settle. Remain in that state for a minute or two.

2   Think about the goals you have set for yourself, and those you are working on; both things that you want to achieve, as well as things to eliminate. Take 1 to 2 minutes to do this.

3   Now, review your day with these two areas in mind, noting where you won and where you have regrets.

4   Think about the successes, while remaining mindful and relaxed, and let yourself enjoy the positive, good feelings that go with that. Enjoy that for 1 to 2 minutes.

5   Next, recall the regrets that came out of the day, and notice what those feel like. See if you can inquire into what happened, and where things went wrong or fell short. Notice how you think about it, breathing into and through the unpleasant emotions or sensations. Note if any amends or reparations might be in order, or if you need to alter your strategy and be more mindful around certain things. Do mindfulness meditation on all of this for 2 to 3 minutes.

6   Remember that tomorrow is another day, and you will have a chance to improve. Try and let all anxiety and stress go.

7   Sit for a few minutes, in regular mindfulness meditation, letting go of all those things that you were working on. Return to your breath, just focusing on the respiration, and allow yourself to calm and settle as you wind down for the evening.

Zero in on tomorrow

TIME: 10 TO 15 MINUTES

When we step into the day's activities, or specific events, without any plans or preparation, our anxiety is higher, and our chances for success are lower. Planning for the upcoming day, even if it's just a simple review of our schedule, can significantly increase our confidence, focus, and productivity and lower our anxiety.

This, like all of the other exercises, is a stand-alone one, and it's also designed to be one in a series, as you build the discipline and skills to create the life that you want, take on a new day, and lower your anxiety.

STEPS

1   Sit in a comfortable work area, where you can review your next day and prepare, as well as relax and settle in for the evening.

2   Sit mindfully and breathe, as you focus and settle. Do this for a few minutes.

3   You may want to do this part with your eyes open. Look at and go over your schedule for tomorrow. What do you notice? Are there some things you look forward to and others that you dread? Make a mental note of that, and breathe into any feelings and sensations that you might have for a minute or two.

4   Review your goals and to-do list. You will likely have another chance to do this tomorrow morning, but go ahead and highlight some of the main items that you want to do tomorrow, as well as the activities you need to do. Take 1 to 3 minutes to do this. See if your anxiety decreases as a result of being more focused and prepared.

5   Do anything else that you need to complete this exercise, such as setting out important papers, an outfit, and so on. Take another minute to do this.

6   Return to regular mindful meditation, with a stable but relaxed focus on the respiration. When the mind and body settle, you can prepare for the rest of the evening.

Gratitude meditation

TIME: 10 TO 15 MINUTES

Gratitude is a really good thing to meditate on, and evening is an especially good time to do it. The day is mostly done, and we had many opportunities during the day. We are fortunate to have this precious human body and the chance to live life fully. It is said that life likes to be appreciated for the opportunities that it avails us, and doing so can enable even more amazing opportunities in the future. This meditation exercise is about doing that, being grateful for our life and opportunities. This practice can diminish anxiety, futility, and boredom, while increasing joy and satisfaction.

STEPS

1 Do this by itself or as a part of winding down and reviewing your day.

2 Find a place where you won't be disturbed and can concentrate and relax. Assume the meditation posture, placing your attention on the breath, as you calm and settle. Stay with this for 2 to 3 minutes.

3 Think about all the things that you have to be grateful for, both the ones that happened today and those in general. Really give it some thought, and try to feel the gratitude or appreciation for all these wondrous things. Take 2 to 3 minutes to do this.

4 Try to take this to the next level and really feel this appreciation and gratitude in your body and in your heart. Try and let it soak in, and then let your gratitude radiate out to others and into life. Stay with this for several minutes.

5 Transition back to regular mindfulness meditation, focusing on the breath and being aware. Stay with this for 2 to 3 minutes.

6 Gently return to your routine, taking some of this sense of gratitude and well-being with you.

Mindful bedtime meditation

TIME: 5 MINUTES

Anxious people often have difficulty going to bed early. This difficulty can be due to the internal energy buzz, or a worrying mind that is turning and spinning, but regardless, they have considerable difficulty choosing a reasonable bedtime and adhering to it. Going to bed earlier and getting more and better sleep can significantly reduce anxiety, as well as improve overall health, focus, and our ability to follow through and be productive.

STEPS

1   Find a comfortable place to relax and settle, while you lightly enter into mindfulness meditation.

2   Think about what might be the ideal bedtime for you, taking into consideration your age, health, nutrition, workload, and any other relevant factors. The first time you do this, you may need to be more formal and extensive as you figure this out. Be sure to include such things as what is the ideal time for you to wake and get up the next day, especially considering your schedule. Take 1 to 3 minutes to do this. In the future, you can likely do this in 30 seconds to 1 minute.

3   Now, think about what usually gets in the way of your adhering to this bedtime—maybe such things as binge-watching a series on Netflix, getting involved in activities on the Internet, exercising too late, eating too late and feeling uncomfortable, or a myriad of other things. Think about what is your usual nemesis. Take 2 to 3 minutes to do this. In the future, it may require less than 1 minute.

4   Return to the mindfulness meditation, watching and following the breath, as you note any significant reactions to what you found. Think about actually planning to go to bed on time and sticking to it. Imagine and feel that for a minute or two.

5   Plan out the rest of your evening to follow the script that you laid out, and take 1 to 2 minutes to do that, as you continue with your mindfulness meditation, then finish your evening.

6   Hopefully, you will follow the script, and get yourself to bed earlier, reducing your stress and increasing your ease and focus.

7   If something else happens, make a note of it and factor it into the next time that you do this exercise. You may want to keep records of this, such as writing sleep times in your calendar or using an app to keep track.

"Be happy in the moment, that's enough. Each moment is all we need, not more."
—Mother Teresa

Chill out: a sleepy meditation

TIME: 5 TO 20 MINUTES

This is one of my favorite meditations for late evening or if I need a short nap during the day.

In our usual meditation, we sit reasonably upright, eyes often open, and focus on remaining quite alert. This meditation exercise is best done in or near bed, often slouching, and with eyes usually closed. You want to calm down and settle your mind, avoid revving back up, and encourage yourself to move into sleep. If it's during the day, you could choose a comfortable chair, slump down in it, and let your eyes close.

STEPS

1   Find a quiet and comfortable place where you can really relax and let go. Make sure you have no place to be for at least 20 to 30 minutes. If it is daytime, you may want to set an alarm.

2   Sit very comfortably, likely slouched, and let your eyes close. Focus on your breath and let yourself really settle and relax. Take 2 to 5 minutes to do this.

3   Don't try to keep your eyes open, and don't try to sit up straight. Get as comfortable as you can, and let yourself relax and let go as much as you can.

4   If thoughts or other things try to arise, just barely notice them and let them go, and keep returning to moving towards dozing and/or sleeping. Take as long as you need.

5   At some point, you will likely begin to doze off. This is a good thing and should not be avoided or resisted. Just keep letting yourself go, taking as long as you need.

6   If it's daytime, when you awaken or your alarm goes off, take a moment to slowly rouse yourself, breathe mindfully for about a minute, and then return to your day.

7   If it's nighttime, you can adjust your pillow and slide down into your comfortable bed, letting yourself continue off to sleep.

Insomnia: tips and a restful meditation

TIME: 10 MINUTES TO AN HOUR OR MORE

Insomnia is a condition that most people experience at some time in their life. Occasional difficulty going to sleep, such as before a big event or medical procedure, is not uncommon and not much cause for concern. It's the regular, ongoing difficulty falling asleep that is problematic and concerning. It can result in depression or anxiety, weight gain, cognitive clouding, immune system suppression, and decreased motivation. Some people have insomnia related to sleep apnea, a condition that can have serious medical implications. Check with your doctor to rule out any medical basis for your insomnia.

I strongly suggest avoiding caffeine or other stimulants, especially after 2 p.m., as this can affect your ability to sleep later.

A regular bedtime that's not too late is best. Also recommended are measures like slowing down in the evening, avoiding stimulation, putting away the electronics, not exercising vigorously or overeating in the evening, and keeping the room dark and not too warm. Failing to follow these measures can lead to a heightened arousal state of the nervous system and make sleep very difficult. If you are prone to insomnia, I suggest doing this meditation before you try to go to sleep.

STEPS

1   If you have tried the approaches listed in the introduction and still can't sleep, your insomnia is likely driven by anxiety. You can verify this by noticing the incessant worrying thoughts. Take a minute or two to become aware of this.

2   Lie on your side and get comfortable. I prefer lying on my right side with the left nostril up, as breathing through the left nostril is less stimulating. While lying on your side, do the basic mindfulness meditation, with an even in and out and a slightly longer exhalation. Do this for 5 to 10 minutes.

3   Find what body area stands out the most, and imagine directing your respiration into and through it. Continue for as long as you need to, and come back into it as needed. Ideally, your mind will slow down, things will shift, and you will ease off to sleep.

4   If you are unable to actually fall asleep, at least you will be getting rest, though not deep sleep. Continue with this as long as you need to.

5   Some sleep specialists recommend getting up to read or watch TV, but something light and not action-packed, instead of lying in bed and worrying about not being able to sleep. Keep the lights low. Writing your thoughts can also be helpful—whether it's a to-do list or a problem to solve—writing it down can transfer ownership from your head to the paper, clearing your mind. Often you can then go back to bed and sleep.

6   If the insomnia is frequent and severe, I strongly suggest that you consult with your medical doctor.

Get back to sleep

Waking up in the night is another unpleasant sleep issue. If your waking up is due to needing to use the bathroom, and you quickly fall back asleep, then it's really no problem. It's when you wake up and have a hard time falling back asleep that it's a real issue. Usually, when this happens, we've awakened with a start, and there is a strong emotion, upsetting thoughts, or a combination of the two. This situation is what we will focus on for this meditation.

STEPS

1   When you wake up unexpectedly the middle of the night or early morning, turn on your side and begin the basic mindfulness meditation. Focus your attention on the breath and do this for 2 to 3 minutes. This simple approach may result in you going back to sleep.

2   If the wakeful state persists, become aware of the primary emotion and sensation associated with it. Focus your attention on that as you breathe into and through it. You can do this for as long as you need to, though it will often shift within 5 to 10 minutes, and you will ease back into sleep. Repeat this as necessary.

3   If it still persists, add some of the cognitive approach and question whether your fearful thoughts are accurate. Continue directing the breath into and through the experience.

4   If all else fails, you may wish to get up for a while to stretch lightly, walk around a bit, journal, read a book, or even watch something light on TV until you can settle enough to go back to sleep.

> "Use every distraction as an object of meditation and they cease to be distractions."
> —Mingyur Rinpoche

PART SIX:
MOVING

Mindful movement

TIME: 5 TO 20 MINUTES

Mindfulness meditation is far more than sitting quietly in a dark room, focusing on one's slowed breathing, and never being disturbed or needing to move. That is a common but incorrect stereotype, and would be very limiting, as we need to be able to be mindful all of the time, and while doing anything. Think about that for a moment because that is the goal. Though this may sound daunting, and it's more a direction than an end state, the first step in integrating mindfulness in our actions is to learn basic mindful movement, so we can have more presence and less anxiety, regardless of what we're doing.

STEPS

1   Sit at your desk or on the side of your bed, someplace where you can mindfully meditate and also stand up and move.

2   Take 1 to 3 minutes to engage in a basic mindfulness meditation with relatively straight posture and awareness of your breath as you follow it. Allow yourself to calm, settle, and focus.

3   Now, look down at your right hand and mindfully move your fingers, being quite aware of the movement. Do this for about a minute.

4   Switch to the other hand and repeat the exercise very mindfully, purposefully moving your fingers. Notice what that's like for about a minute. Next, do both hands at the same time.

5   Next, repeat these steps using your feet; first one, then the other, and then do both at the same time. Take a couple minutes to complete this.

6   Now, sit where you can readily get up. Return to the essential mindfulness breathing for 30 seconds to 1 minute, then mindfully stand up very slowly, paying close attention to what it feels like as you move each muscle and make each movement. Take a minute or so to do this.

7   Once you're standing, pause briefly and then reverse the process sitting down. Again, move quite slowly and mindfully, bringing attention to every movement. Then sit for about a minute, noticing how it feels.

8   Finally, add the breath to your movement. Inhale as you stand up, then exhale as you sit down.

9   Slowly, mindfully, as you stand up, inhale, pausing for a moment at the top, and then slowly, mindfully sitting as you exhale.

10 Sit for 1 to 2 minutes, and then make any notes that you wish.

Mindful walking

TIME: 10 TO 30 MINUTES

This next exercise is a mainstay at mindfulness and Vipassana meditation retreats. If you have ever gone on one of these retreats, you've undoubtedly encountered this exercise. It's quite simple really, though not so easy. The aim is to carry mindfulness into walking and is done in a slow, deliberate manner. This exercise generally follows a period of sitting, often 45 minutes to an hour, but can also be done anytime. While this develops mindful awareness while walking, it also enhances balance and grounding.

STEPS

1   Start with the Basic mindfulness exercise (page 18). Sit with the spine straight but relaxed, following the breath of the nostrils or another place, and let everything relax and settle. Stay with this exercise for at least 5 to 10 minutes. Let yourself really settle in.

2   If your eyes are closed, open them for at least a minute while you continue meditating before you begin the walking.

3 Stand mindfully, as you learned in Mindful standing (page 71). Remain standing for at least a minute, making sure you're oriented and stable.

4 Very slowly raise your foot, being aware of each movement, and slowly take a step forward, then slowly lower your foot. Stand there for a moment, maybe 30 seconds.

5 Now repeat with the other foot, slowly and mindfully raising it, moving it forward, lowering it, and then pausing briefly. Notice how that feels.

6 Please remember, the goal is not to walk someplace or traverse a certain distance. Rather, focus on taking extremely mindful steps, regardless of how far you actually walk.

7 Continue this for as long as you like, being aware not to speed up, start rushing, or get distracted.

8 If you should wish to take it to the next level, there are many options. You can start with your right foot, as one option, as it is considered dominant according to Taoists (even if you're left-handed). You can also try inhaling as you lift your foot and move it forward, then exhale as you place your foot down and settle. When they first begin, some people like to count one number for each step that they take. Try various forms and see what appeals and what is most helpful.

Mindful cooking

Mindful cooking can be a bit challenging because cooking can be complex and more challenging to do mindfully. It can still be done with practice. Mindful cooking is a good exercise because we have numerous opportunities every day to practice this at home, whether with something as simple as making a cup of tea, all the way up to a multicourse meal. It's suitable for mindfulness practice as well as reducing anxiety. As you go about this meditation, prepare your food in a slower, more focused, and conscientious manner. Pay particular attention to each step.

STEPS

1   Go very slowly starting out; with practice, most things can be done at near-average speed, while still remaining quite mindful.

2   Sit at the table, and begin with your basic mindfulness meditation. Continue until you feel focused and settled, and then extend it for a minute or two.

3 Gather the food and utensils you'll need, going slowly and paying careful attention. Then, sit or stand for a moment and return to simple mindful breathing.

4 Begin to prepare the food, taking great care as you wash and slice the vegetables, prepare the starch and meat, and so on. Go slowly and pay attention. Pause as needed to do 30 seconds of mindfulness meditation.

5 The cooking phase can present some challenges, as it can involve the stovetop, the oven, and multiple dishes simultaneously. Just do your best, and try not to get too rushed, distracted, or lost. You will improve considerably over time. Pause as needed to return to mindful breathing.

6 In the end, sit for a minute or two and regather your calm and focused awareness.

7 You may wish to make some notes or suggestions regarding your experience.

"Mindful eating is a way to become reacquainted with the guidance of our internal nutritionist."
—Jan Chozen Bays

Mindful eating

TIME: 10 TO 30 MINUTES

Mindful eating can be useful for many things: to develop conscious awareness and focus, lose weight, reduce dyspepsia, and make mealtimes a more settling experience. Mindful eating is another everyday activity at meditation retreats, as well as at monasteries. Like the other activities in this series, it's done slowly and with much focus. You are also encouraged to really taste and enjoy the food as you eat it; something that is often missed in daily life and frequently leads to overeating, unwanted weight gain, and anxiety. By the way, when we eat slowly, we usually consume less. This is because the signals from the stomach regarding fullness and blood sugar level have more of a chance to reach the brain and tell us when we are full or satisfied.

STEPS

1 Sit at the table and look at the food in front of you. Pause and then do 30 seconds to 2 minutes of mindful awareness.

2   Notice if you are hungry and if you want to rush and overeat or if you are relatively calm.

3   One by one, choose the items that you're going to eat, and pay particular attention to how much you take, while noticing if your thoughts are encouraging you to take more than you really want or need. Breathe into, through, or with the experience, and stay with it for at least 30 seconds.

4   Choose an appropriate amount of food, and slowly dish it onto your plate.

5   Move to the next item and continue the process, until you have all the things you're going to eat on your plate.

6   Choose your first bite and slowly gather it onto your utensil and move it into your mouth. Don't rush.

7   Chew it thoroughly, really noticing and relishing the taste, and swallow slowly.

8   Continue loading your utensil, moving the bite to your mouth, chewing slowly and swallowing, and noticing your level of fullness, until you are finished. You may pause as needed in this process and take 30 seconds to 1 minute for a mindfulness refresher.

9   At the end, sit for a minute or two to reflect upon the experience.

Mindful dishwashing

TIME: 5 TO 25 MINUTES

This mindfulness meditation activity follows naturally from the previous ones and is often a favorite one for retreat participants. I used to get this activity at retreats because I wasn't an excellent cook, but I sure knew how to wash dishes. As with the other exercises, we will clean the dishes in a slow, deliberate, mindful manner, taking care not to drop any dishes, and ensuring they are clean. It's pretty simple and straightforward.

STEPS

1   Sit for 1 to 3 minutes and establish your essential mindfulness.

2   Gather the dirty dishes from the table and stove and take them to the sink area. Remember to do this mindfully, pausing as needed to refresh your mindfulness.

3   Arrange the dishes in the order you will wash them, then pause for 30 seconds or more and breathe before you begin.

4   Grasp and lift one dish at a time, scrubbing carefully and thoroughly, looking at it without being distracted, and then rinse it. Pause for a moment and breathe, then repeat.

5   These are the necessary steps. Repeat them, trying not to get lost or distracted. You can do the same sort of thing later when you put the dishes away.

6   In the end, take 1 to 2 minutes, breathing mindfully and feeling the satisfaction of mindfully completing the job. Notice if you had/have less anxiety doing the job mindfully.

Mindful driving

TIME: 5 TO 30 MINUTES OR LONGER

Imagine what a different world it would be if everyone was a mindful driver. Most drivers are not very mindful at all; they engage in speeding, rolling through stop signs, following too closely, not signaling lane changes, even texting. Mindful driving is about reducing your anxiety by becoming a better driver in general and thus adding increased calm to your travels. This exercise uses adherence to traffic laws and slowing down to effect positive changes to driving skills and increase our ease and calm. I've used this exercise many, many times, and my driving and sense of ease when driving have improved considerably.

STEPS

1   If you are uncertain about any of the traffic laws where you live, review them first.

2   Get seated in the car, seatbelt buckled, mirrors adjusted, and ready to drive. Now, take at least 2, but not more than 5, minutes to do the basic mindful meditation. Keep your eyes wide open the entire time.

3   Start the car and get ready to pull out. Do so very mindfully.

4   Follow all the traffic laws, which will require careful observation of signaling, turns, stopping distance behind other cars, speed, and so on. Also, breathe in an even fashion. Please do not get lost in your breathing; primarily pay attention to your driving and the rules of the road.

5   Notice how you feel about this and any thoughts you may have about driving lawfully. The first time I tried this, it felt so prolonged, and I kept wanting to drop my mindfulness, speed up, and revert to my usual driving pattern. See if you have a similar experience.

6   Continue with this exercise as long as is comfortable or practical. Come back to this exercise as often as you wish.

7   If you get too distracted and start speeding up, you can always pull over in a safe location, place the car in park, and return to your basic mindfulness meditation for 1 to 3 minutes with your eyes open, and then begin driving again.

8   At the end of your drive, return to basic mindfulness meditation for 1 to 2 minutes, review your experience, and make notes if you wish. Congratulate yourself on integrating mindfulness meditation into your daily life. Over time, this type of exercise can significantly reduce anxiety and stress associated with driving.

> "Mindless fear is greater than mindful fear."
> —Idowu Koyenikan

An effective meditation for fear of flying

TIME: 20 MINUTES TO SEVERAL HOURS

The fear of flying is a common anxiety, and I have successfully worked with dozens of clients on this over the years. Sometimes it's just flying in general, but usually, it is more specifically linked to takeoff, landing, and turbulence. If you have a fear of flying, pause for a moment and think about what part of flying it's related to. Also, think about if it reminds you of a particularly bad experience, and what the thoughts are that go along with this. Statistically, as you probably already know, the actual risk of being involved in an airplane accident is very, very low.

STEPS

1   Preparing for this particular anxiety before the actual flight is good. I suggest starting to work on it at least the night before, if not several days before the trip.

2   If you have a scheduled flight and are feeling anticipatory anxiety, choose a time to work through your feelings, find a place to relax, sit in a meditative posture, and begin to follow your breath and settle for 1 to 3 minutes.

3   When you're reasonably relaxed, begin to think about flying—either the flight you're going on, one that you've been on that stands out, or just flying in general. Take 2 to 3 minutes to do this.

4   When the anxiety reaction arises, let the thinking stop and move your attention and awareness to the anxiety, both emotionally and physically. Just breathe into and through this, calmly and gently. Stay with this for quite a while, up to 10 minutes. Notice if there is a shifting or lessening of the symptoms.

5   You can repeat this part of the exercise as many times as you want or need to.

6   If it's the actual day of the flight, try to have a stress-free day leading up to it. Get enough sleep, eat a good breakfast, leave for the airport with lots of time, and avoid caffeinated or stimulating drinks.

7   Engage in lots of proper, slow breathing, as you slowly make your way through the airport and to the gate. Stay aware of your lower abdomen, feet, and hands, so you stay more grounded as you continue to breathe slowly and deeply. Do this on and off, and as much as you can, especially as you are waiting to board.

8   As you board, move slowly and deliberately, maintaining your focus
    on the slow, deep breathing, and the awareness of your body. Try and
    control your thoughts, reminding yourself of the statistical safety of
    what you are doing. Focus on these things, doing your best not to let
    your thoughts start spinning, thus avoiding getting caught up in scary
    thoughts. You can distract yourself with a conversation with a seat-
    mate, for instance, to keep your mind occupied. Use whatever works
    for you.

9   Maintain this approach, throughout the flight, and especially during
    moments that you are most apt to fear, such as takeoff, landing, and
    turbulence. Try to maintain your body awareness, then your deep,
    slow breathing. Keep reminding yourself, if necessary, of your relative
    safety, as you continue with the deep breathing and body awareness.

10 When you land, deplane slowly, maintaining deep breathing and
    awareness. Congratulate yourself on your success, and remind your-
    self again of the relative safety of flying. Quick side note: if the anxiety
    is exceptionally intense, please see a medical professional. You may
    need medication and psychotherapy to assist you.

Stuck in traffic

When caught in traffic, many people get anxious about the number and closeness of the cars, the traffic congestion, and being somewhere on time. This is actually an excellent time to do centering and relaxing mindfulness meditation. Driving offers a unique opportunity to focus on breathing, especially into your lower abdomen, and relaxing. The more centered and relaxed you are in traffic, the safer a driver you are, and the time passes more quickly. Awareness of your lower body helps with grounding and relaxing. You can also work with your breathing, a simple balanced three or four count, and just stay present. This exercise helps me become relaxed, grounded, calm, and present.

STEPS

1 When you are driving, if you notice yourself becoming anxious, make a mental note of this and focus your breath into your lower abdomen. Also be aware of the feeling in your hands and feet, to make sure that you are present and remain so.

2   Use light awareness of the breath into the lower abdomen while keeping most of your attention on driving.

3   Lightly breathe into the lower abdomen as you drive. You can count to three or four as you breathe if you are able without being distracted from your driving.

4   Just stay with this light awareness of your breath in the lower abdomen and the even in and out of the breath if you're able, and drive as you usually would. This should lower your anxiety, as you drop your center and relax.

5   If you notice you are distracted, simply return to the breath in the lower abdomen.

6   One key, crucial thing to remember when utilizing any form of mindfulness meditation while driving a car: You must maintain your primary attention on safely driving the car. This is not the time to get too relaxed or spaced out, so please be mindful of your ability to do this type of exercise while driving, and discontinue the exercise if necessary.

Overcoming test anxiety

Many people have test anxiety—I used to be one of them. I can relate to the anxiety and dread that rises up inside and clouds the mind, making it so difficult to remember what you need to recall to perform well. A little bit of alertness and being on edge is good, though, and actually improves our performance. However, once we get over that optimal level of activation or alertness, we see a steady and significant decrease in our abilities. Just like in meditation, you want to be alert and also very relaxed.

STEPS

1   You can do a significant amount of work to reduce your test anxiety long before the actual test. Refer to the initial steps in the exercise regarding fear of flying (page 177) and utilize those to do some desensitization before the real exam.

2   Be well prepared. One essential step in reducing and controlling our anxiety around a test involves really knowing the material that will be covered, or practicing and getting proficient at the skills in a movement test. Having that internal confidence that "you can do this" goes a long way in reducing your anxiety.

3   Prepare for the test, as much as possible, in precisely the same conditions as the test itself. It's called state-specific learning and means we're more likely to remember material and skills when in the same circumstances that we learned them. This is very important and often overlooked.

4   In the days and weeks leading up to the test, study and practice the material repeatedly and in shorter sessions. The night before and the day of the test, study a lot. The combination of these two types of preparation provides the best results.

5   The day of the test, prepare and keep yourself as calm and relaxed as you can, much like the steps covered in the exercise on fear of flying.

6   Before you go in for the test, or as you sit there waiting for it, do the basic mindfulness meditation; sitting up straight but relaxed, hands resting in your lap or on the desk, focusing on the balanced breath with longer and slower exhalation, and keeping your thoughts neutral if not positive. Begin this at least 5 to 10 minutes before the test, and continue it during the exam.

7   Focus on one item at a time, and do not let your mind race ahead. If you get to a thing that you don't know, just notice it and breathe, but try not to judge it. Stay calm and relaxed. It can be useful to pause 30 seconds to 1 minute between items, if you have the time, to help maintain a slow and calm pace.

8   Go through the ones you're reasonably sure that you know, and then go back through to complete or double-check the others. Try not to get caught in second-guessing yourself, going over ones you probably successfully answered, ruminating on them, and changing them to an incorrect answer.

9   Keep breathing, on and off, and keep settling yourself as you go through the test. Pace yourself, and try to stay out of negative thinking.

10 When you leave, you might wish to go for a short mindful walk, feeling your body and breathing slowly and deeply as you direct the breath into and through any remnants of anxiety or stress. The more you practice this, the less fear you'll have.

Mindful public speaking

TIME: 10 TO 20 MINUTES

Public speaking is one of the most common fears in the general population. As a person with a stutter, I can guarantee you that you can get over this anxiety, as I now really enjoy public speaking instead of dreading it. This is another one of those areas where the better prepared you are, in terms of knowing the material, the more relaxed and successful you're likely to be. Know your content so well that you can focus on the relaxing and speaking.

STEPS

1   Start your day with solid preparation to ensure that you are as physically steady as possible. Eat well, be well rested, and begin your day with at least a brief mindfulness meditation.

2   Particularly with public speaking, since you are already anxious and a bit on edge, avoid caffeine. Caffeine is virtually certain to imbalance you or significantly detract from your performance.

3   When you are in the room where you will be speaking, sit and do the basic mindfulness meditation for at least 5 to 10 minutes. During this time, focus on the long slow exhalation, to allow yourself to settle as much as you can.

4   I recommend looking at the desk or floor in front of you to reduce distractions and allow your mind to be more open and relaxed. Do this for at least 2 to 3 minutes.

5   When it is your turn to speak, start slowly and don't rush or "speed stress" yourself. That only induces anxiety. Try to lightly follow your notes, pausing to look up and out and connect with the audience. See if you can find a friendly and kind face to connect with. This can significantly lower your anxiety.

6   Pause between main ideas, even for a few seconds, to return to this lower deep breathing. Do this for as long as you are speaking.

7   When you're done with the speaking, try to remain there for a moment, unrushed and more relaxed. Do not rush into sitting down or leaving. You are the speaker, and you are in control. Try to remember to carry this slower and calmer pace throughout the entire event.

8   As you stand or sit, getting ready to leave, return to body awareness and mindful breathing. Take as long as you need given the time that you have.

9   You may wish to make notes regarding the event and what things seem to help.

"Let the breath lead the way."
—Sharon Salzberg

PART SEVEN:
5-MINUTE

Relax and settle the breath

TIME: 5 MINUTES

When we're anxious, our breath gets out of whack. The fastest and most direct way to affect our anxiety is by altering our breathing, and this is the most effective way to breathe to quickly reduce our anxiety.

STEPS

1   You can do this sitting, standing, or lying down. Ideally, I suggest sitting.

2   Sit relatively straight but relaxed. Look down, to reduce your visual stimulation and distractions.

3   Slowly inhale for a count of three to four, then exhale for a count of five to six. You may wish to pause at the bottom of the exhalation for a count of one or two.

4   As you do this, you will likely notice a calming and settling effect, and it can happen fairly quickly.

5   Continue to breathe in this manner, letting the calming and settling effect deepen.

6   Try to focus on the breathing and let your thoughts subside.

Circular breathing

TIME: 5 MINUTES

This mindfulness meditation exercise, called the microcosmic orbit breathing, comes from Taoism and is excellent for calming oneself, balancing one's breath and energy, and clearing one's mind. It's quite simple, yet it can be quite profound, both in reducing anxiety and increasing spiritual awareness.

STEPS

1   Sit or stand, and breathe with your mouth somewhat open. It is suggested to have your tongue touching the ridge behind your front teeth. Tilt your head slightly forward to straighten your spine and especially your neck.

2   On the inhalation, imagine the breath and energy rising from the base of the spine, up to the top of the head. Pause there for a moment. Some practitioners feel a fullness in the head and increased mental clarity. It's okay if you don't feel that or if you feel something else.

3   On the exhalation, imagine the breath and the energy coming down from the top of your head, much like a waterfall, until your attention rests in the lower abdomen or ideally at the base of the genital area, the perineum. Pause for a moment and let yourself settle.

4   Just continue to repeat this cycle; on the in breath, go up the spine to the top of the head, and on the out breath, go down the front to the perineum area.

5   Do this as many times as you comfortably can during this 5-minute exercise. Pause if you feel spacey or ungrounded.

Shoulders and breath: keys to releasing tension

TIME: 5 MINUTES

When we are anxious, our shoulders tend to rise and tense, and we often hold our breath. Both of these actions are virtually guaranteed to maintain or even increase anxiety. We can significantly reduce our anxiety by mindfully working with and reversing these two patterns.

If you're self-conscious, do this one when you are alone.

STEPS

1   Sit forward, in a chair or on the side of the bed. Let your arms dangle at your sides. Keep your back fairly straight, but relaxed, and breathe with your mouth open.

2   As you take a nice full inhalation, let your shoulders rise and fall repeatedly, as your arms and hands shake things out.

3   After a nice full inhalation that includes bouncing the shoulders up and down and shaking out the arms, let out a quick and complete exhalation. Let the shoulders and arms drop completely as you do this. This is a form of letting go.

4   Some practitioners like to add a mental component to the letting go, by adding a "So what?" on the exhalation.

5   Keep going through the exercise repeatedly until you are ready to conclude. After the last "letting go," just feel the release and relaxation, and rest in it.

Worry ruminations: getting unstuck

When we are anxious, we often ruminate, going over and over the fears in our head and replaying what we dread. Like a car stuck in snow or sand, our spinning thoughts are just getting us more and more stuck. We need to get unstuck from our worry ruminations.

STEPS

1   The perfect time to do this exercise is when we're stuck in our worry thoughts, unable to resolve the issue, and don't know what else to do.

2   Notice the worry thoughts, going around and around, and how frantic we are to get some relief. Notice what the narrative, or story, is that we keep telling ourselves. Get clear on it.

3   Notice the emotion or feeling that goes with this story. Once you have that, acknowledge it.

4   Find the body area or physical experience that goes along with the thoughts and the emotion.

"I am an old man and have known a great many troubles, but most of them never happened."
—Attributed to Mark Twain

Notice and stop negative thinking

TIME: 5 MINUTES

In psychology, there is a time-tested technique called thought stopping. Just like it sounds, it is designed to stop negative thinking, especially when our thoughts are incessant and scary. Letting them run on and on is not useful and just makes things worse. When we notice our ongoing negative thinking, we can speak to ourselves in ways to reduce or even stop the negative thoughts. When you notice you are having negative thoughts that are ongoing and not helpful, use this exercise.

STEPS

1   Be aware of your negative thinking and the destructive effect that it is having.

2   Notice that negative thoughts are like a loop, playing over and over, and if left unchallenged, they will continue.

3 Decide to do thought stopping, and with resolve and clarity, tell your thoughts to "Stop," speaking either aloud or to yourself. Be firm about it. You can also add shifting your thoughts to something else that is more pleasantly attention-grabbing.

4 Repeat it as many times as you need.

5 Try to get your mind to a more open or neutral state.

Sit with the emotion to decrease worry

TIME: 5 MINUTES

One way to stop incessant worry is to shift our attention to what emotion goes with it. It is often the underlying emotion that is fueling the rampant worry, so shift your attention from your worry thoughts to simply being aware of the emotion that goes along with it, and your worry and anxiety will significantly decrease.

STEPS

1   When you become aware that you are caught in worry thoughts, this is the ideal time to do this exercise.

2   Notice what the worry thoughts are or what the story is that you're worrying about.

3   Ask yourself, "What is the emotion that goes with this?"

4   Identify the emotion, and simply be aware of or feel it.

5   Continue for as long as you have or as long as it takes. You can always come back to it later. Notice how the anxiety and rumination abates when you make this shift.

Feel the fear to reduce the anxiety

TIME: 5 MINUTES

In the previous exercise, we discovered how making the shift from worrying thoughts to the emotion underneath them can significantly reduce our anxiety and worry. Making a similar shift from the worry thoughts and rumination to the physical sensation that goes along with it can also significantly reduce anxiety. Focusing on the sensation may affect and reduce anxiety and rumination more than feeling the emotion.

STEPS

1   When you notice yourself being anxious and caught up in worry, this is the ideal time to use this exercise.

2   As soon as you notice the worry thoughts, ask yourself, "What is the sensation that goes with this?"

3   Identify the main physical sensation that you are having; maintain awareness of it, and breathe. This could be tightness in your chest, tension in the throat, nausea in the stomach—whatever sensation stands out the most.

4   Stay with the sensation as long as you are able. You can always come back to this later.

5   Be aware of the reduction in anxiety and worry.

Take a mindful walk

TIME: 5 MINUTES

A short, mindful walk is an excellent way to help break the cycle of anxiety and create ease and well-being. It doesn't have to be long; just maintain awareness of your walking, feel your feet on the ground, and breathe as you walk. Let your head clear, focus, and relax.

STEPS

1   When you need a break and can walk a bit, even just down the hallway or around the building, this is an ideal exercise.

2   Stand up, mindfully inhale, and begin to walk.

3   Keep your breathing balanced and feel your feet as they alternately touch down on the ground.

4   If you need spaciousness and inspiration, keep your head up.

5   If you need to settle and focus, keep your gaze down.

Distraction challenge

This short exercise has become one of my new favorites. I use it to hone and strengthen my focus, especially if I'm feeling scattered or easily distracted. Difficulty focusing is common when anxious. I select an area to sit or stand where there are things that would ordinarily distract me, such as cars or people. I work to combat these distractions to strengthen my focus.

STEPS

1 Find a place to sit or stand where there are numerous objects moving by.

2 Notice the objects as they go by and how your attention naturally follows them, leaving you distracted.

3 Choose something in your visual field that you are going to maintain your gaze and focus on, and try not be distracted. It should be on the other side of the passing distractions.

4   Start the exercise, exerting will and discipline to maintain your attention, without following the various objects passing by.

5   Notice any internal thoughts, reactions, or resistance. Maintain your focused awareness of your surroundings.

6   When done, notice your increased ability to focus.

Traffic light meditation

TIME: 5 MINUTES

This is my all-time favorite driving exercise. Driving affords us numerous opportunities to practice meditation and stay calm. This exercise utilizes sitting at a light as an opportunity for a brief period of meditation. Be sure to continue paying attention to the traffic around you, the light, and your surroundings. Do not get lost in meditation. Simply use this as a way to breathe and stay in the moment.

STEPS

1 Be prepared to do this exercise when you stop at a traffic light. You don't know how long or short the signal will be, so be flexible.

2 When you stop, gaze at the sky slightly above or below the traffic light. Let your attention be both focused and a bit relaxed.

3 Make sure your primary attention is on the traffic light and driving safely. Please do not ever lose your focus or awareness while driving.

4   Slowly breathe in and out as you do the mindfulness meditation gazing at the sky around the traffic signal. This should help you relax as you wait for the signal to change.

5   Enjoy the meditation and decreased anxiety. Notice when the light changes and mindfully proceed with driving. Don't use this meditation when you plan to turn at a traffic light; only use it when you are going straight.

> "One is a great deal less anxious if one feels perfectly free to be anxious, and the same may be said of guilt."
> —Alan Wilson Watts

PART EIGHT:
DO
ANYWHERE

Standing in line

TIME: 2 TO 30 MINUTES

I do this exercise frequently when I am out of the house and around town. It seems that there are always lines to wait in and sources of anxiety, hence an opportunity to do a little inconspicuous mindfulness meditation. It's also excellent for integrating mindfulness into everyday life. It works like this: When I find myself standing in line, such as at the grocery store, I center myself while standing, and then I find an open or empty spot to rest my gaze. While doing this, I become mindful of the breath and continue to follow it as I stand, waiting for the line to move. I can increase my calmness, patience, mindfulness, and integration, all without anyone noticing.

STEPS

1 The first thing, of course, is to remember to do this exercise. While you are shopping, you might want to remind yourself that you're going to do this when you go to check out. You can even select a line where you will need to wait.

2 As you stand in line, feel your feet underneath you, try to find your center, and then notice your breathing. How long you do this depends on how long you will be standing there.

3 Find an open area to lightly and openly gaze at. I find this approach effective in this type of situation as it allows the attention to be more relaxed and not caught up in the visual details around you.

4 Just stand there in a centered and balanced manner as you follow your breath and allow your gaze to be open and spacious. Stay aware of your breathing and the relaxed gaze, but also maintain at least a little bit of attention to the line and its movement. You don't want to space out or seem odd.

5 As the line moves, proceed with it, and keep returning your attention to your awareness of your breathing and your relaxed gaze.

6 If you get distracted, return to your centered standing, focused breathing, and relaxed gaze.

7 When you're all done, you may wish to review the exercise and how it went. Reflect on whether it decreased your stress and anxiety and helped increase your calmness and patience.

Sitting and waiting

TIME: 5 TO 20 MINUTES

We all do a fair amount of sitting and waiting, and this can be anxiety-provoking. We might feel anxious because we're waiting for some news that might be difficult, because there are others around and we have social anxiety, or simply because we feel anxious when we sit with nothing to occupy us. Instead of reaching for your smartphone to dash off a hurried text or catch up on the latest bad news, do a simple mindfulness exercise.

STEPS

1   As you sit there, think to yourself, "I'm going to do a little mind-fulness meditation." Stay with this intention instead of grabbing your smartphone.

2   Notice any anxiety or stress that you might feel just sitting quietly and mindfully meditating. Take 30 seconds to 2 minutes for this, and breathe into and through any stress symptoms that may be rising.

3   Adjust your posture so your back is relatively straight but relaxed, and follow your breath. Do this for 2 to 3 minutes.

4   If you need something to gaze at, try the bare floor in front of you or an empty bit of wall.

5   Once you're there, sitting and waiting, just continue to be aware of your breath going in and out. If you feel anxiety or stress, just be mindful and breathe into and through it.

6   If you need a little break, you can take one every 5 to 15 minutes. Just relax for a minute or two, then reestablish your mindfulness.

7   Do this exercise for as long as you need—it largely depends upon how long you are going to be waiting. Once while waiting at the DMV, I had 45 minutes to do this exercise, and it greatly alleviated my anxiety and stress.

8   At the end, take a minute to review how you did and the results.

Feel your body and breathe

TIME: 20 SECONDS TO 30 MINUTES

This is the most basic and accessible mindfulness meditation that you can do. I've honed this one over 35 years of practice. You can do it anywhere, and it's the one I used when I was lost underwater scuba diving and also when I felt paralyzed by fear while rock climbing.

This mindfulness meditation uses awareness of your body, and ideally your main physical sensations, in combination with simple breathing. It uses the most simple and fundamental elements of some of the longer and more complex meditations and is designed for immediate and real-world stressful situations.

This is one of those exercises that you must remember to do for it to work. It's also good to practice it so that it becomes relatively automatic when it comes time to apply it. Just as with the martial arts, you practice these moves over and over, so the response is reflexive when you need it. This exercise involves only two elements: feeling and being aware of your body and breathing.

1   This exercise can be done anytime and anywhere, so practice it often. Anytime you think of it, pause and take a moment to "feel your body and breathe." Maintain the focus on your body awareness and the breath for at least 30 seconds and up to 2 to 3 minutes. This is essential.

2   You can do this repeatedly in a single meditation session, getting in multiple rounds of pausing to feel your body and breathe for 30 seconds to 2 minutes, and then take a short break of 30 seconds to 2 minutes before you begin again. Some people find it helpful, at least in the beginning, to mentally or verbally say to themselves, "feel my body and breathe."

3   There is a second phase of this that incorporates the more ideal level of the exercise. When you feel your body, focus on a specific area, the area that stands out the most. With the breathing, imagine directing the breath into and through that particular body area.

4   Now you have the essential exercise as well as the more ideal exercise. I suggest you practice both in the manner described in steps two and three. You should also note, however, that under significant duress, the best you are likely to be able to do is to have general body awareness. This is just fine and to be expected.

5   In addition to formal practice sessions, it's good to do this exercise at random times, such as when you stop at a stoplight, stand up or sit down, open a door, and so on. When you are practicing in this manner, simply take 30 seconds to 1 minute to feel your body. The more repetitions that you can get in, the more quickly you'll build the reflexive response and your proficiency.

6   From time to time, reflect on how you are doing with this exercise. You may wish to make some notes. You can also enlist family and friends to startle you to see how you respond.

Accept whatever is happening

TIME: 2 TO 20 MINUTES

This is another relatively simple and straightforward exercise that has enormous benefits in its simplicity. One thing that keeps us stuck, frustrated, and anxious is that we have situations and feelings occurring that we are not just observing and allowing to exist. We resist, fight, get angry, get anxious, get sad, and generally wish things were a different way. Though a typical human response, this is a recipe for keeping things stuck. We don't have to agree with or like what's going on, but we do need to be with it just as it is.

STEPS

1   Sit with the back straight and relaxed, and follow the in and out of your breathing at the nostrils or another place. Allow your mind to settle, taking 2 to 3 minutes.

2   Think about something that's been bothering you, something that you have some history with and that feels stuck. Take 1 to 3 minutes to do this. Continue with your meditative breathing as you do this.

3 Notice what you have been resisting. What is it that you don't want to accept or feel? It might be that someone no longer loves you, that you don't make enough money and prospects don't look favorable, or worries about your health, and so on.

4 After you have identified what you have been resisting, try to simply be aware of it, without judging, blaming yourself, or getting caught up or lost in it. This step is essential. Take 1 to 3 minutes to work with this.

5 Try to simply feel the emotion, breathe with it, and notice the physical location and sensations that go with this. Breathe with, into, or through the experience. Take several minutes to do this. It may not be pleasant, and that's okay. Try to have compassion for yourself.

6 In the end, simply sit for 1 to 3 minutes, and notice if the distress around it has lessened, and if so, how much. This exercise may need to be repeated multiple times, especially for stubborn issues. Do not despair, and have kindness and compassion for yourself.

7 Sit for about a minute before resuming your day. Return to this as often as needed.

"Mindfulness isn't difficult, we just need to remember to do it."
—Sharon Salzberg

Metta for yourself

TIME: 5 TO 30 MINUTES

Metta, meaning loving-kindness and compassion for ourselves, is a beautiful thing. This exercise can be done anywhere, and is especially useful if we're feeling a little down, self-critical, or disappointed in ourselves. Whoever we are and whatever we have done, we still deserve self-love and kindness. It is a healing gift that we can give ourselves.

STEPS

1 Find a quiet place where you won't be disturbed, assume the meditative posture, become aware of your breath, and settle yourself. Sit quietly for 1 to 3 minutes.

2 As you are sitting and meditating, think of yourself and say silently or aloud:
May I be filled with loving-kindness. May I be safe from danger, outer and inner. May I be well in body, mind, and spirit. May I be happy and peaceful.

3 Do this for 2 to 3 minutes.

4   Notice if you can let in the kind and loving thoughts and how that feels. Take a minute or two for this.

5   If you get stuck or can't let something in, notice what that is and breathe into and through it for 1 to 3 minutes.

6   Sit for 30 seconds to 2 minutes, and then go about your day.

Metta for others

TIME: 30 SECONDS TO 5 MINUTES

While it is quite useful to be able to conjure up loving-kindness for ourselves, it is equally valuable, and sometimes more challenging, to feel that same sort of loving-kindness for others. It's stressful when we can't feel love towards others, and it is of great use to able to rectify that. That is why we practice this. Numerous daily opportunities can happen anytime and anywhere, allowing us to practice and develop this vital, loving-kindness for others. If you need to practice the more detailed version of this, you can do so by following the steps in the previous exercise, and substituting *others* for *yourself*.

STEPS

1   When you find yourself having negative thoughts of ill will, malice, or harm towards another, recognize that this is an excellent person to practice loving-kindness towards. It is a particularly useful exercise to do regarding ex-spouses, those that you may feel have harmed you, or individuals and/or groups for whom you feel prejudice or bias.

2   As soon as you notice the negative thoughts or feelings regarding someone, try to stop the negative thinking and attitudes towards them. Just be aware of the pattern and stop it. Take 10 seconds to a minute to do this, and see if you can shift into "neutral." Take another 30 to 60 seconds to try and rest in this neutral position.

3   Once you have stopped, or at least allayed the negativity, and are resting in the neutral zone, it is time to call forth the loving-kindness for them. See if you can do this, even if it's only a small amount. Take a few seconds up to 2 minutes to do this.

Find inspiration and calm in nature

Meditation on nature can be a very healing exercise, as it naturally generates increased relaxation and openness, and it is mostly non-conceptual, so our thinking mind is calmed. Many Eastern religions use meditation on nature as a way to bring about a more open and spacious state of mind, and most Westerners love to spend time in nature. It doesn't even require a dramatic experience for it to be beneficial. Just glancing out the window at the sky, grass, or trees, even for an instant, can be inspiring and calming.

STEPS

1 This exercise, designed to be done anywhere, can take as much or as little time as you have. The longer you spend, the better your experience is likely to be.

2   Wherever you are, see if you can see a little nature; it might be a bit of sky out the window, the grass and trees outside, or something more expansive and inspiring. Whatever it is, allow your eyes to gaze at it as you follow your breath and become calm and settled. Spend as much or as little time as you have.

3   If you get distracted, you can come back to the breath and gaze at nature. Try to clear your mind of thoughts, and focus more on the naturalness and beauty. Try to breathe a little more deeply and slowly, seeing if you can deepen your state of ease.

4   This is a great way to "take a little break" and clear your mind and settle.

5   When you're done, return to your day, and see if you can take a little bit of the comfort and ease with you.

"Mindfulness is simply being aware of what is happening right now without wishing it were different; enjoying the pleasant without holding on when it changes (which it will); being with the unpleasant without fearing it will always be this way (which it won't)."
—James Baraz

Take a bathroom break

Funny title, right? You will soon understand why. Sometimes we find ourselves in a very stressful situation, and we need to break away, but it seems that there is no way out. The longer we have to endure it, the more anxious and stressed we become. I'm going to give you a simple way to get yourself a physical and mental break from those demanding situations. Simply say, in whatever words work for you, that you "have to use the bathroom." Everyone understands this and is unlikely to deny you. It gets you out of the stressful situation, so you can take a few minutes to apply some calming exercises before you return.

STEPS

1   When you find yourself in a stressful situation and need a break, this is the ideal time to do this exercise. You may find yourself a bit anxious in preparing to use this, and if so, take 30 to 60 seconds to breathe and then proceed.

2   In whatever words work for you, tell them that you are sorry, but you must step out for a few minutes and use the bathroom. It can be useful to begin standing up and move towards the door as you announce this.

3   Keep moving, don't wait for approval, and walk out the door. You may wish to mumble something like, "I'll be right back."

4   Once outside, you can go to the bathroom and sit in a stall, where you can apply more formal meditation techniques. Some people prefer to walk around a bit instead of sitting, though this runs the risk of some-body seeing that you didn't actually go to the bathroom.

5   Wherever you go, do some calm centered breathing and elongate the exhalation, with a short pause at the end. Try to feel your center, the lower abdomen, and be aware of your hands and feet. All of these things should help you calm and settle in the shortest amount of time.

6   When you feel calmer, slowly return to the situation, focusing on your calming breath and centering as you walk.

7   When back in the situation, try to continue the exercise, gazing down as needed, and still focusing on the longer, slower exhalation.

8   Later, you may wish to make some notes as to how it went.

Ask yourself: true or false thoughts?

TIME: 45 SECONDS TO 10 MINUTES

Significant stress and anxiety can come from thoughts that are simply not true. In clinical psychology, we may call these cognitive distortions, negative thinking, or catastrophic thinking, depending on the degree of negativity. The end result is that these negative thoughts frighten us and make it difficult to function. We need to get a grip on these thoughts, and one of the first ways to do this is to become aware of them and then ask ourselves if they are really true.

STEPS

1   If you find your mind spinning and notice that you're getting increasingly upset and anxious, look at your thoughts and what they are. They are likely quite negative and scary. Make a note of this. This can take as little as 30 to 45 seconds.

2   Try to be aware of and feel the emotion and physical experience that goes with the negative thinking. This can take 30 seconds to 2 minutes.

3 Notice what negative thoughts you are having, and begin to inquire into and question the validity of them. This can take 1 to 3 minutes. Look directly at the thoughts and ask yourself, "Are these thoughts really true?"

4 You can do this with a central negative thought or a series of them. A series will take longer to work with.

5 As you expose the non-validity of the thoughts, your anxiety should decrease. Make a mental note of this.

6 As a next step, think about the more uplifting reality of the situation for 1 to 3 minutes.

7 Congratulate yourself. This is a pretty complete cognitive therapy intervention that you have just done. Sit for up to a few minutes, depending upon how much time you have. Make some mental or physical notes, and resume your day.

100

Encourage yourself

TIME: 3 TO 10 MINUTES

This mindfulness meditation exercise is an excellent stand-alone or as an adjunct to the previous exercise. In the last exercise, we used a cognitive intervention for negative thinking and to discover what was the accurate perception of reality. In this exercise, we have the opportunity to move beyond that and encourage ourselves. This is sometimes known as positive thinking, which has been shown to help reduce anxiety, improve mood, and encourage action. Two caveats go with this approach: keep it within the realm of reality/possibility, and support it with action. We all need a coach to encourage us, be it external or internal. In this exercise, you will develop your inner coach.

STEPS

1   As a way to retrain your brain and self-talk, this can be used anytime and anywhere. If you've been negative and have gone through the cognitive exercise in the previous activity, you can add this to the end of it.

2   In this exercise, we will assume that it is stand-alone and will use it to enhance and reprogram our self-talk in general.

3   Begin with basic mindfulness meditation and get yourself into a relaxed and settled state. Take 1 to 3 minutes to do this.

4   Think of an area where you are often self-critical. Notice what kind of thoughts or internal self-statements you have and how they make you feel. Notice the emotions and body sensations that go with it. Take 1 to 3 minutes to do this.

5   Think of some genuinely positive and kind things to say to yourself. Talk to yourself like a loving coach or parent would. Give yourself encouragement and speak in ways that motivate you to move forward. Take at least 3 minutes to do this.

6   Notice how good it feels to have a kind and reassuring voice, soothing you and urging you to move forward. Stay with this for a minute or two.

7   Sometimes when you first begin doing this, the words may ring hollow. Just breathe and stay with it; continue to speak in soothing and encouraging ways to yourself, and then take actions to move forward.

8   In the end, just sit in basic mindfulness meditation for a minute or two. Make any notes that might be useful, and then resume your day.

> "If you want to conquer the anxiety of life, live in the moment, live in the breath."
> —Amit Ray

225

FURTHER READING
and RESOURCES

Books

Pema Chödrön's books

How to Meditate: A Practical Guide to Making Friends with Your Mind

The Places That Scare You: A Guide to Fearlessness in Difficult Times

When Things Fall Apart: Heart Advice for Difficult Times

Jon Kabat-Zinn's books

Mindfulness for Beginners: Reclaiming the Present Moment—and Your Life

Wherever You Go, There You Are: Mindfulness Meditation in Everyday Life

Mingyur Rinpoche's books

The Joy of Living: Unlocking the Secret and Science of Happiness by
Yongey Rinpoche Mingyur and Eric Swanson

Joyful Wisdom: Embracing Change and Finding Freedom

Tsokyni Rinpoche's books

How Mindfulness Works

Open Heart, Open Mind: Awakening the Power of Essence Love

Echkart Tolle's books

The Power of Now: A Guide to Spiritual Enlightenment

Websites

Mindful.org

Tergar.org

BeingFullyHuman.org

WhatMeditationReallyIs.org

Tricycle.org

EMDR.com

MBCT.com

GettingThingsDone.com

Brendon.com

INDEX

ACKNOWLEDGMENTS

It is only fitting that I start at the beginning and acknowledge the many mindfulness teachers that I was fortunate to meet and study with, who gave me an excellent foundation in mindfulness meditation. I also greatly appreciate several faculty members at the Institute of Transpersonal Psychology who introduced me to integrating clinical psychology and meditation. Great appreciation to the many Tibetan teachers, and especially the Great Masters that I had the great fortune to engage with, particularly my first Teacher. For my wife, Padma, who is brilliant, loving, caring, awake, and lovely. You are the love of my life. Thank you for your ongoing love, encouragement, and support. Finally, for my best friend, Paul Sibcy, the finest friend I've ever known. Thank you for your love, friendship, understanding, and encouragement over the many years.

ABOUT *the* AUTHOR

MICHAEL SMITH, PHD, is a licensed clinical and transpersonal psychologist in private practice in Longmont, Colorado, just outside of Boulder. He has earned master degrees in general-experimental psychology, counseling psychology, transpersonal psychology, and a doctorate in transpersonal psychology. He also holds numerous certifications in EMDR and areas of somatic psychology. Michael has been teaching mindfulness-based meditation and psychotherapy since the late 1980s. He taught mindfulness-based courses at the graduate level for over 15 years at the Institute of Transpersonal Psychology and Naropa University and has spoken on this topic at numerous conferences. He has practiced many forms of meditation since the late 1960s, most notably mindfulness meditation and Dzogchen Tibetan Buddhism. He has been an authorized meditation instructor for over a decade. Michael has participated in a vast number of sports and outdoor activities and holds rank in several martial arts, which he studied for decades. By combining multiple power therapies in his work, he gets more rapid therapeutic results while teaching clients how to integrate these modalities into their daily life. You can learn more about Michael and his work at DrMichaelSmith.org.

CPSIA information can be obtained
at www.ICGtesting.com
Printed in the USA
LVHW020325280819
629091LV00001B/1/P